Battlegr

POZIERES

The photograph shows Mouquet Farm after the Australians, Canadian and British assaults. The view is from the back buildings, looking over the courtyard and remains of main buldings towards the position formerly held by the Australians, all of whose reliefs had to descend the distant slope, often in plain daylight.

Battleground Europe

POZIÈRES

Graham Keech

Series editor
Nigel Cave

LEO COOPER

First published in 1998 by
LEO COOPER
an imprint of
Pen Sword Books Limited
47 Church Street, Barnsley, South Yorkshire S70 2AS

ISBN 0 85052 589 6

A CIP catalogue of this book is available
from the British Library

Printed by Redwood Books Limited
Trowbridge, Wiltshire

*For up-to-date information on other titles produced under the Leo Cooper imprint,
please telephone or write to:*

Pen & Sword Books Ltd, FREEPOST, 47 Church Street
Barnsley, South Yorkshire S70 2AS
Telephone 01226 734555

Cover painting: **The First Buckingham Battalion at Pozières 1916** *by Wollen.*
Reproduced Courtesy of the Director, National Army Museum, London.

CONTENTS

Australian pioneers at work behind the trenches previous to the Great Advance. TAYLOR LIBRARY

INTRODUCTION BY SERIES EDITOR

This latest volume in the Battleground Europe series is the first about the 1916 Battle of the Somme which does not have as its starting point the dreadful day of 1 July. It is a welcome development, always planned, but quite a long time in the coming.

For well over half a century much of the interest of the British public has been fixed on that fateful day. It is an understandable human reaction to what happened to Britain's volunteer army on the first occasion that it was launched into a major action. Unfortunately this preoccupation has resulted in the neglect of the rest of that battle, which went on for some four and a half months, and indeed it has been argued to the neglect of what happened to the British and Dominion armies over the remaining two and a half years of war. This has resulted in a failure by most to realise what an extraordinary evolution that the British land and air forces underwent in this time span; academics now concentrate on the very steep learning curve that the army underwent, culminating in the victory of 1918, itself possible the most underwritten of any of Britain's military success stories. The reasons put forward for this lack of interest and the concentration on the disaster of 1 July are numerous and there is no time to rehearse them here; suffice to say that this series aims to move on from the more well worn paths of the visitor and pilgrim and on to other areas where casualties were, undoubtedly, very heavy, but where success and cogent military planning were far more common, though certainly not the rule.

Pozières is a typical Somme village, strung out along the famous Albert-Bapaume road, an early objective of the offensive. It is on a high spot, and rarely is it possible to stand on the site of the windmill of such ill repute without a stiff breeze blowing. The ground round and about, certainly to the east of the village, is something of a plateau, although the eye deceives and cannot see the small undulations and ripples that formed such a vital part of both the attack and the defence.

The fighting around Pozières lasted for some six weeks, though it had played a part in the battle from its earliest days, standing as it did above the British and German Front lines on 1 July. It involved a number of Imperial (that is British) divisions, but its name is of immortal memory to Australia, three of whose divisions (1st, 2nd and 4th) fought long and hard here through the summer days of the latter end of July, August and early September.

Graham Keech gives a full description of what happened on the ground, and the large number of maps makes it possible to follow what happened on the ground in some detail. Devoid of many physical features, this will be an invaluable aid for many of us who have puzzled over just what did happen here, and brings about some understanding of the heroic achievements of those men over eighty years ago. The description also helps us to understand something of the German military mind, how her generals determined to fight the battle and illustrates that suffering on the Great War battlefields was far from being a uniquely British activity. The German soldier was a most formidable fighting man.

With the enormously increased interest in the Great War in the last decade or so, it is now becoming clear that Australia and New Zealand could both do with a museum that can show just what their armies achieved in the war. The Australian War Memorial is, I am told, an outstanding museum. But there is very little on the fields of battle that portrays something of the fighting quality of these men from so many thousands of miles away; nothing that explains why they came, nothing about their vital contribution to the victorious British army of 1918. Travel is now so much easier and cheaper that it is not unusual to find visitors from 'down under' visiting these far away places in Flanders and Picardy whose names still sound with resonance on regimental standards and in the national consciousness.

In recent years the South African and Canadian governments have spent large sums of money to ensure that the memory of their men is kept alive. They have provided wonderful educational opportunities for people from all over the world to have a better understanding of a conflict whose nature is extremely difficult for many to comprehend. It must be admitted that in recent years Australia also has provided new memorials, such as at Bullecourt, Passchendaele and, most recently, Mouquet Farm. There is the excellent museum at villers Bretonneux, close to the national memorial to the missing Australians in France. Yet this is off the well beaten track of so many visitors to the Western Front, and at the extremity of the operations of Anzac. Perhaps a site at Pozières would be most ideal; not much further than a ninety minute drive from all the great points of Australian and New Zealand arms -Villers Bretonneux in the south, Mont St Quentin, Flers and Pozières on the Somme, Bullecourt on the Hindenburg Line, Fromelles in French Flanders, Plugstreet and Messines Ridge just inside Belgium and of course the immortal Salient, Polygon Wood and Broodseinde Ridge and the fields around the deeply moving Tyne Cot cemetery and memorial.

These men deserve not only to be commemorated but to be understood – for commemoration without education is of limited value. It is to be hoped that something can and will be done about this in the near future, before the memory of Anzac is confined to plaques, headstones and memorial walls in the green fields of Flanders.

Nigel Cave

Ely Place, London

INTRODUCTION

Pozières lies on the highest part of the Somme battlefield **(See map 1)**. It was to be captured on the first day of the battle, 1 July 1916, but in the event did not fall until almost another month had passed. By then its name, along with those of many other small, insignificant French villages, was well known to the inhabitants of the United Kingdom. When Australian troops finally reached the site of the mill and the main German lines on the far side of the village they were unable to identify them, the effects of the artillery bombardments had been so devastating. The First World War has been called a war of artillery and nowhere is the truth of that statement better illustrated than at Pozières. The shells fell, day after day, on both sides until nothing was left that could be called habitation. The Australian Official Historian, C.E.W. Bean, was convinced that that the divisions involved at Pozières were subjected to greater stress than in the whole of the Gallipoli campaign. *'The shelling at Pozières did not merely probe character and nerve; it laid them stark naked as no other experience of the Australian Imperial Force ever did.'* The legacy of the battle can be felt even now. The name Pozières is to many Australians synonymous with incompetence and mistrust of British generals in the war.

The village today is very much as it was in 1914. It lies on either side of the Roman road from Albert to Bapaume, the greater part on the left. On the right the line of building quickly gives way to open ground, from where the Australians attacked in 1916. The railway lines, which played such an important part in the fighting, are no more, but in places their remains can still be detected. With the aid of the trench map **(See map 5)** most of the important features of July and August 1916 can be identified.

General Birdwood meets some of the Australians in a wood after the battle.
TAYLOR LIBRARY

The fighting for Pozières and Mouquet Farm was so intense that it is impossible to recount every action. The main events have been covered and reference made to some of the subsidiary actions. To make the best use of this book it should be read through to familiarise the reader with places, names, events and maps. This done, it is hoped that the reader will feel sufficiently interested to visit the village and follow the tours to the various sites. Don't forget to take the book with you for easy reference.

The final section gives some suggestions for further reading.

ACKNOWLEDGEMENTS

No book on the battles of the Somme would be complete without reference to the War Diaries of the units involved. When using these primary sources one cannot but wonder, where and under what conditions they were written, what was the writer like, did he ever consider that his work would be read and quoted eighty years on? I am indebted to all these authors and to the staff at the Public Record Office at Kew who have assisted me with accessing these records.

I wish to express my thanks to the Trustees of the Imperial War Museum for permission to reproduce certain photographs from their collection. The photographs concerned are identified by their catalogue numbers either Q or E(Aus). I am also grateful to the IWM staff, particularly Peter Simkins for information concerning Albert Jacka, Ian Carter for his advice and help with the photographs and all members of the reading room who supplied me with reference books and maps.

I would also like to thank Derek Butler and Mrs Christine Woodhouse of the Commonwealth War Graves Commission, Maidenhead for their help with the loan of cemetery registers and the Commission for leave to reproduce register maps and diagrams.

I am also grateful to Ralph Whitehead (New York) for German document translations; Jenny Nairn (Largs, Australia) for details and the photograph relating to Arthur Blackburn; and Trevor Pidgeon for the aerial photographs of the Chalk Pit, Mouquet Farm and Brind's Road. Finally, my thanks to the series editor, Nigel Cave, for his help and advice during the preparation of the manuscript and for the aerial photographs of Pozières village and the Australian Memorial at the site of the mill.

ADVICE TO TRAVELLERS

Before setting out on your trip to the battlefields a few simple preparations can pay dividends. As with all foreign travel you are advised go fully insured. For reciprocal medical cover you need a form E111, which can be obtained from Post Offices. Full personal insurance and breakdown cover for your car can be obtained through the AA or RAC. In addition, obtain a Green Card from your insurance company to extend your car insurance for the countries to be visited. The individual company concerned will provide full details. Purchase a First Aid kit and ensure that your tetanus immunisation is up to date - it is very easy to get scratched on rusty metal or wire when walking on open land. Wartime relics, such as shells grenades etc, are all dangerous and should never be touched or moved.

In my experience it nearly always rains at some time during a battlefield tour. Go prepared for wet and cold weather. Heavy shoes or a good pair of boots are recommended as the ground can get very muddy and there are often ruts and holes which can lead to accidents.

To make the best use of your time on the battlefield a picnic lunch is suggested. There are no problems getting provisions at supermarkets in Albert or Bapaume but don't forget to take a knife (Swiss Army) and maybe some drinking utensils. If you prefer to have a break for lunch the Poppy Restaurant, on the D929 Albert-Bapaume road at La Boisselle serves a good one but get there early, it gets very busy.

Getting to the Pozières battlefield is relatively easy. It takes less than two hours on the Paris motorway from Calais. Leave the A1 at junction 14 (Bapaume). In the town follow the signs for the D929 road to Albert. The IGN Green Series maps numbers 1 and 4 are very detailed; the Michelin numbers 51,52 and 53 less so but still useful.

Accommodation is available in Albert, Bapaume and in some of the nearby villages. However, you do need to consider transport to and from Pozières if you do not have your own. A full list of all types of accommodation can be obtained from

Comite Regional du Tourisme de Picardie, 3 Rue Vincent Auriol 80000 Amens Tel: 00 33 322 91 10 15.

The following short list may prove useful.

Hotels:

The Hotel de la Paix, 43 Rue Victor Hugo, 80300 Albert.
Tel: 322 75 01 64

Hotel de la Basilique, 3-5 Rue Gambetta, 80300 Albert.
Tel: 322 75 37 00

Bed & Breakfast

Sommecourt, 39 Grand Rue, 80300 Courcelette.
Tel: 322 74 01 35 Paul Reed and Kieron Murphy.

Les Galets, Route de Beaumont, Auchonvillers 80560
Tel :322 76 28 79 Mike & Julie Renshaw.

10 Rue Delattre, Auchonvillers 80560
Tel: 322 76 23 66 Avril Williams.

MAPS

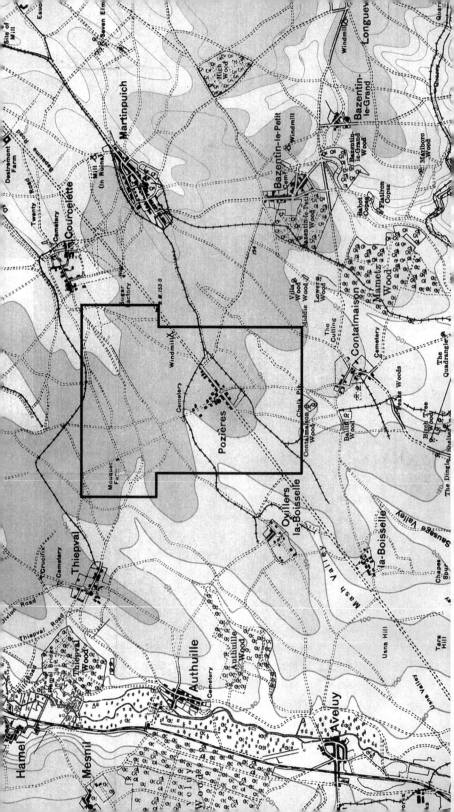

Chapter One

THE OPENING PHASE
JULY 1916

Pozières: 1 - 20 July

The German Front Line in the region of Pozières was almost at right angles to the Roman road running from Albert to Bapaume **(See map 2)**. From a position in front of Thiepval, it ran south-east through a westerly projection (the Leipzig Salient), across the valley in front of the village of Ovillers La Boisselle (Ovillers) and thence across the road. It continued in the same direction in front of La Boisselle and on towards Fricourt. The German Second Line ran parallel with the First but approximately 2500 to 3500 yards behind it. It passed from Grandcourt, through two redoubts, The Stuff and The Zollern and on

German trench photographed in April 1916 before the Somme Battle.

THE SOMME, 1916
THE BATTLE OF ALBERT 1ST JULY
THE FOURTH ARMY OBJECTIVES

N

Map 2. Objectives 1 July 1916. (Based on Official History Map).

to Mouquet Farm before passing behind Pozieres, through what was the highest point on the battle field, the Pozières mill. It then crossed the road and continued on towards the villages of Bazentin le Petit and Bazentin le Grand.

When the Fourth Army attacked on 1 July their final objective for the day, in the area under consideration, lay just behind the German Second Line from Grandcourt to beyond Mouquet Farm, where shortly after it dipped southward to take in the northernmost part of Pozières village before crossing the road and passing on towards Contalmaison. The capture of Pozières was the responsibility of the 8th Division, Major-General H. Hudson, a regular division which was the left division of III Corps, Lieutenant-General Sir W.P. Pulteney. The Corps was positioned on the forward slopes of a long low ridge between Albert and La Boisselle. Major features of the location were hills and valleys on either side of the Albert to Bapaume road. Looking towards Bapaume, Usna Hill and Mash Valley lay on the left, and Tara Hill, Sausage Valley and Avoca Valley on the right. At the head of Mash valley lay the village of Ovillers La Boisselle whilst to the south between the road and Sausage Valley lay La Boisselle itself.

8th Division

The division had a particularly difficult task as in their sector not only were the two front lines well separated, up to 750 yards in places, but the line of attack was threatened, on the right, by the German salient at La Boisselle, in the centre by the highly fortified village of Ovillers and on the left by the Leipzig Salient **(See map 3)**. The division depended to a large extent on the success of the two adjacent divisions, the 34th to the south and the 32nd to the north.

During the night of 29/30 June the divisional infantry moved into their assembly positions as shown below, with 23 Brigade nearest the Roman road and 70 Brigade in front of Le Bois de la Haie (known to the British as Authuille Wood).

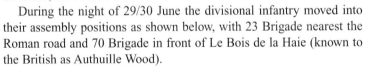

Right	Centre	Left
23rd Inf. Brigade.	**25th Inf. Brigade.**	**70th Inf. Brigade.**
In Line: 2/Middlesex.	In Line: 2/Royal Berks.	In Line: 8/KOYLI.
2/Devons.	2/Lincolns.	8/Yorks & Lancs.
Support: 2/West Yorks.	Support: 1/Royal Irish Rifles.	Support: 9/Yorks & Lancs.
Reserve: 2/Scottish Rifles.	Reserve: 2/Rifle Brigade.	Reserve: 11/Sherwood Foresters.

Shortly before zero hour, 7.30 a.m. on 1 July, the assaulting battalions of 23 Brigade (2/Middlesex and 2/Devons) took up positions on No Man's Land in Mash Valley. Their objective was to reach the

15

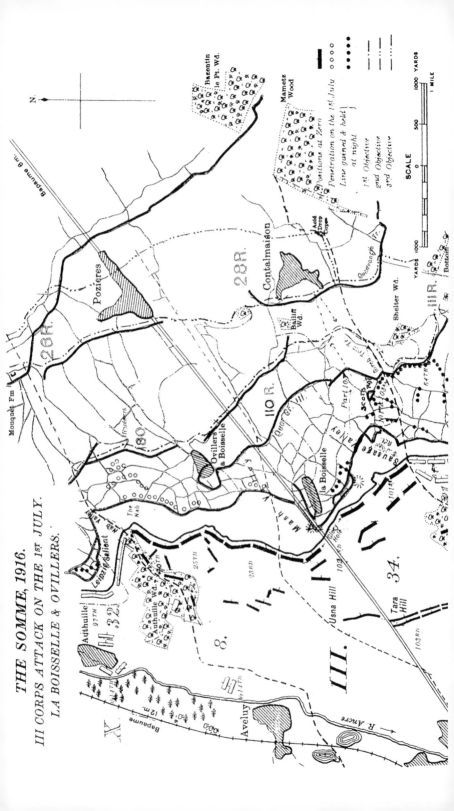

THE SOMME, 1916.
III CORPS ATTACK ON THE 1st JULY.
LA BOISSELLE & OVILLERS.

Roman road and then move up it to take Pozières. When the barrage lifted they moved forward and managed to reach the German front line and later passed over to the support trenches but were quickly repulsed. So great were the losses, mainly from machine gun fire from La Boisselle, that in spite of an attempted reinforcement by 2/West Yorks, the Middlesex could only hold on until 9.15 a.m. At this time they retired into No Man's Land where the survivors lay until, under the cover of darkness, they returned to the starting line. A similar fate befell the 2/Devons who were hit by direct fire from Ovillers and flank fire from La Boisselle. A few reached the German line but after a determined fight they were forced back into No Man's Land.

In the centre, where the object was to take the trenches around Ovillers, 25 Brigade fared little better. On the right the 2/Royal Berkshires managed to gain the German line but in insufficient numbers to hold it and they were soon bombed out. In the fight their Commanding Officer, Lieutenant-Colonel A.M. Holdsworth, was mortally wounded. On the left the 2/Lincolns managed to capture about 200 yards of front line and were in touch with parties of the King's Own Yorkshire Light Infantry (KOYLI) of 70 Brigade on the left. Efforts to move forward to the next line of trenches failed and, although some of the later waves of the 2/Lincolns had now also reached the German line, such was the level of the enfilade machine gun fire and the effect of continual bombing attacks that by 9.00 a.m. they were forced to retire to their start line.

In an attempt to retrieve the situation, both the support [1/Royal Irish Rifles] and the reserve [2/Rifle Brigade] tried to move up, but suffered heavily from the accurate enemy barrage and were also hampered by the state of the communication and front line trenches. The leading company of the 1/Irish Rifles did manage to get as far as the German support line but in turn were forced back; the 2/Rifle Brigade were never able to reach their own front line.

On the extreme left 70 Brigade attacked up the southern slope of Nab Valley to capture the German Second Line and Mouquet Farm. For some unknown reason the enemy barrage was initially less heavy on their front, which permitted the 8/KOYLI, and the 8/York & Lancs to reach the German front line in numbers. Here, on the left, the 8/KOYLI were held up by enfilade fire but in the centre the attack moved forward to the enemy support and reserve lines, then disaster struck. The retirement of the 2/Lincolns lead to a mistaken belief that a general withdrawal was underway. The 8/KOYLI, mixed with some elements of the 2/Lincolns, retired to the start line. Here they met the support battalion, 9/York & Lancs coming forward. Like the support and reserve battalions of 25 Brigade, they had been badly mauled in reaching their own front line. However, together with the 8/KOYLI, 2/Lincolns and 8/York & Lancs they moved forward and regained the German front line and in the centre moved to the support line. This in turn led to an extremely perilous situation, since both flanks were exposed to the heavy machine gun fire from Ovillers and Thiepval. The reserve battalion, the 11/Sherwood Foresters, tried to move up at 8.40 a.m. but they too were hampered by the enemy barrage on their lines and by the machine gun fire in No Man's Land. They never reached the German front line.

By 10.00 a.m. the shattered remnants of the infantry units were either pinned down in No Man's Land or back in their own lines under heavy and persistent bombardment. Some few remained in the German lines, but as the day progressed it was unclear whether they retained their hold or had been overcome. Before any further attack was possible another artillery barrage was deemed to be necessary, but the commanders were loath to call this up whilst unsure of the fate of their own troops in the German lines. At 7.00 p.m. orders were received for the relief of the division, to be replaced by the 12th Division.

In the course of the day's fighting the casualty figures were staggering. 70 Brigade suffered the heaviest losses, including two Commanding Officers, Lieutenant-Colonel. B.L. Maddison who is buried in Blighty Valley Cemetery, Authuille and Lieutenant-Colonel A.J.B. Addison who lies in Becourt Military Cemetery. Altogether the division lost 200 officers and 4908 other ranks, killed, wounded or missing.

34th Division

As already mentioned, if the 8th Division was to be successful it depended to a large extent on the adjacent divisions, and in particular the 34th. This division, to the south, was also part of III Corps **(See map 3)**. The main thrust of this division was to be on the Fricourt Spur and in Sausage Valley to include La Boisselle. It was then to advance to within 800 yards of the German Second Position at Pozières, where it was to join up with the 8th Division. The right would be turned back to the south of Contalmaison to form a defensive flank towards Mametz Wood.

The Commander of the 34th Division, Major-General E.C. Ingouville-Williams, 'Inky Bill' to his troops, elected to commit all twelve of his battalions in the initial assault. They were drawn up in four columns of three battalions each, on a 400 yard front. The troops in line and support were drawn from 101 Brigade, Brigadier-General R.C. Gore, and 102 Brigade, Tyneside Scottish, Brigadier-General T.P.B. Ternan. The Reserve was made of 103 Brigade, Tyneside Irish, Brigadier-General N.J.G. Cameron. In this case the term Reserve was somewhat of a misnomer as the units were all to move forward together. The two columns of the 102 Brigade were separated by a larger gap to permit them to attack on either side of La Boisselle.

La Boisselle Village

20/N.F.	21/N.F.	10/Lincs.	15/R.Scots.
23/N.F.	22/N.F.	11/Suffs.	16/R.Scots.
25/N.F.	26/N.F.	24/N.F.	27/N.F.

102 Brigade	101 Brigade
+	+
two battalions 103 Brigade	two battalions 103 Brigade

N.F. = Northumberland Fusiliers.

As part of the overall strategy for the July 1 attack a number of mines were exploded under the enemy lines. Three of these were located on the 34th Division front and each was exploded at 7.28 a.m., two minutes before zero hour for the attack. The first of the mines, containing 40,000lbs of the explosive, ammonal, was just to the left of the Albert-Bapaume road under a strong point which jutted out from the front line Y Sap. The second, at Inch Street, just beyond the Glory Hole, contained two charges each of 8,000lbs. Further south the largest mine, Lochnagar, contained 60,000lbs of ammonal and was again positioned over a strong point, the Schwaben Höhe.

To achieve the general thrust previously mentioned the division had three specific objectives: the German front and first reserve lines, the German intermediate line and the line east of Contalmaison. Each objective was to be taken by the corresponding wave in the plan of attack i.e. the third objective was to be taken by the units of 103 Brigade. La Boisselle itself was not to be taken directly but by two bombing parties who were to detach themselves from the leading waves on either side of the village and move sideways as the battalions moved forward.

At zero hour, under heavy artillery and machine gun fire, the leading battalions moved forward into No Man's Land and then those following moved down the Tara-Usna ridge. On the extreme left the 20/Northumberland Fusiliers and 23/Northumberland Fusiliers were practically wiped out. According to *The Thirty Fourth Division 1915-1919* Lieutenant-Colonel J. Shakespear:

> *'thinner and thinner the trail extended into the German lines, and amongst those who had penetrated furthest were found the bodies of Lieutenant-Colonel Lyle 23/Northumberland Fusiliers and Lieutenant-Colonel Sillery 20/Northumberland Fusiliers, where they always wished to be, at the head of their battalions'*

The two Lieutenant-Colonels are buried next to one another in Bapaume Post Military Cemetery, Albert.

The 25/Northumberland Fusiliers following up also lost heavily in a vain attempt to carry the attack into No Man's Land. South of La Boisselle the third column managed to reach the German third line, Alte Jäger Strasse, in front of Quergraben III, but as numbers dwindled and, under constant attack, they were forced to retire to the second line, Kaufman Graben. In the meantime a mixed party of troops from all three brigades established itself on the Lochnagar crater. In their number was Lieutenant-Colonel Howard 24/Northumberland Fusiliers who there died of his wounds. After dark these two groups managed to make contact and to consolidate their positions.

On 101 Brigade front the two right hand battalions, 15/Royal Scots and 16/Royal Scots, suffered heavy casualties and were forced off line into the area allocated to the 21st Division. In so doing they left uncaptured two strong points, Scots Redoubt and Sausage Redoubt (also known as Heligoland). Eventually realising their mistake they managed to move to their left and captured Scots Redoubt next day. By midnight 1/2 July the remnants of the brigade were holding Wood Alley down to Round Wood. In contrast, on the left of the brigade front, the 10/Lincolns, and the 11/Suffolks, forced to attack a re-entrant in the German line, were cut down by machine gun fire from Sausage Redoubt and La Boisselle village. They suffered so badly that for all intents and purposes they ceased to exist after the initial assault

Lieutenant-Colonel W. Lyle and Lieutenant-Colonel C.C. Sillery. Bapaume Post Cemetery Albert.

and following this setback the 24/Northumberland Fusiliers were held in the front line.

By nightfall only isolated gains had been made, La Boisselle had not been captured and overall it seemed unlikely that the division could hold that little it had. In the course of the day the division lost 264 officers and 6097 other ranks killed, wounded or missing.

Having exploited all his reserves, Ingouville-Williams had to call upon the 19th Divison in Corps Reserve to take La Boisselle. Orders to that effect were received by the division on the evening of 1 July, and the village or, more correctly, pile of rubble, was finally secured on 4 July. In the course of this action the division was awarded two Victoria Crosses: Lieutenant-Colonel Adrian Carton de Wiart commanding 8/Gloucesters and Private Thomas Turrall, 10/Worcesters.

Lieutenant-Colonel L.M. Howard. 1/Tynside Irish, Ovillers Military Cemetery

Meanwhile the 34th division was able to achieve some minor adjustments to its position, but was in no state to launch a major attack. On 5 July it was reconstituted. 102 and 103 Brigades were transferred to the 37th Division and replaced by 111 Brigade (Brigadier-General R.Barnes) and 112 Brigade (Brigadier-General P.M.Robinson) from the same division.

Given the situation at the end of 1 July the Commander-in-Chief, Sir Douglas Haig, was anxious to build on the limited successes achieved. Accordingly, he ordered that the attack should be pressed in the area between the junction with the French forces north-east of Maricourt and a point half way between La Boisselle and Contalmaison, whilst leaving the enemy in the area to the north of the Albert-Bapaume road under constant pressure. On 2 July the 17th Division captured Fricourt and during 3 and 4 July Bernafay and Caterpillar Woods were taken. As already mentioned, the 19th Division succeeded in capturing La Boisselle on 4 of July and the outskirts of Contalmaison were reached on 5 July. On 7 July the 17th, 23rd, 19th and 38th Divisions embarked upon the capture of Contalmaison village and Mametz Wood which, with the exception of a portion of the northernmost part of the wood, were captured after three days of heavy fighting. Trônes Wood was attacked and partially taken by the 30th Division on 8 July and by 13 July Mametz Wood had been cleared by the 21st Division. With these gains Haig was in a position to attack the German second line system including Pozières.

In preparation for an attack on the German Second Line, General Sir Henry Rawlinson, with the support of his divisional and corps commanders, arrived at a plan to attack at dawn when the poor light would restrict the view of the enemy machine gunners. Haig did not agree with the idea and proposed that instead of attacking on the whole front simultaneously, XV Corps should attack in the evening, supported by III Corps, to establish a line from Contalmaison Villa to the spur north-east of Marlborough Wood. The attack by XIII Corps would follow at daybreak on the following day. On 12 July, following representations from Rawlinson in which he relayed his satisfaction with the plans and preparations for a dawn attack, Haig changed his mind and confirmed the morning attack. Troops were to be moved up into the line during the night and the attack would take place at 3.25 a.m. after an intense but short (5 minutes as opposed to the usual 30 minutes) bombardment. He also suggested that supporting trenches should be dug by XIII Corps on the southern slopes of the Longueval-Bazentin ridge and that the flanks were to be secured by taking and holding Trônes Wood and Mametz Wood. For the attack, finally set for 14 July, the first objective was the German front and second trenches from Delville Wood through Longueval as far as Bazentin le Petit Wood. The second was a line embracing Delville Wood and Longueval and passing behind Bazentin le Petit village.

Gun captured in Mametz Wood. TAYLOR LIBRARY

A newly hollowed-out shelters for reserves at Mametz, July 1916. Note large screw pickets on the left. In trenches similar to this the 1st Australian Division relieved a portion of the British troops before Pozières on 20 and 21 July. TAYLOR LIBRARY

Whilst the above operations were being carried out the 34th Division had not been idle. Following its reconstitution, and the replacement of the 18/Northumberland Fusiliers by the 9/North Staffs, it went into Corps reserve. On the night of 8/9 July 58 Brigade of 19th Division was relieved by 112 Brigade and on the following night 111 Brigade completed the relief of 56 Brigade of the same division. At 4.00 a.m. on the 10th Major-General Ingouville-Williams formally took over command from Major-General G.T.M. Bridges.

On 10 July both brigades were ordered to assist the 23rd Division in its attack on Contalmaison by attempting to occupy a line from the north-west corner of that village to a point on the Albert-Bapaume road about 1200 yards from the western end of Pozières, an advance of 600 yards. Unfortunately, the German artillery laid down a heavy barrage on the front line just at the time of the projected advance and, in the resulting confusion, orders cancelling the attack were delayed and heavy casualties were sustained by 13/Rifle Brigade. On the following day both brigades managed to gain a line 200 yards into No Man's Land which was extended by further efforts on 13 July. Also on the 13th the division extended its line to the right, taking over ground from the 1st Division up to the north-west corner of Contalmaison.

On 14 July **(See map 4)** the division was ordered to gain ground towards Pozières village. The village was at that time under artillery bombardment from a number of units and it proved difficult to arrange and co-ordinate a lift to permit a position to be established from which to assault the village. Eventually at 6.00 p.m. a platoon of 111 Brigade and two of 112 gained a footing in a trench about 200 yards south of the village. However, by 10.00 p.m. it was learned that they had been ejected by the enemy and a defensive machine gun line was set up. An attempt to retake the trench, by two companies of the 8/East Lancs failed. On the following day the division was to attack and occupy the village from the south using 112 Brigade. Assuming success, 111 Brigade was to pass through to attack the Second Line at the windmill adjacent to the Albert-Bapaume road. Whilst this attack on the village was carried out the 1st Division was to advance from the western edge of Bazentin le Petit Wood astride the Second Line east of Pozières. The 1st Division attacked at 9.00 a.m. followed 20 minutes later by 112 Brigade which advanced in artillery formation. As the first three battalions passed Contalmaison Wood they split into two companies forward and two companies fifty paces back, forming six waves. The remaining battalion, the 10/Loyal North Lancs, were used to carry ammunition and bombs to form a dump in the Chalk Pit on the track running up to the orchards on south-west corner of the village. The attack went well until the leading waves were within 400 yards of the

German shells bursting on the British lines, near Trônes Wood.

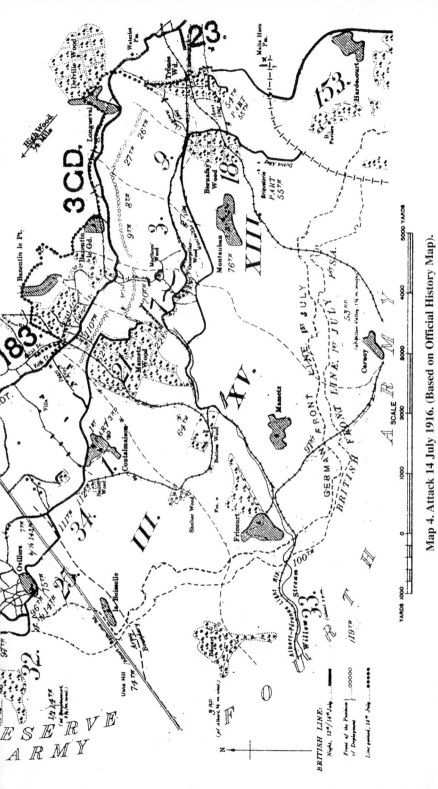

Map 4. Attack 14 July 1916. (Based on Official History Map).

The Chalk Pit on the track up to Pozières. Visited by Major-General Ingouville-Williams 15/7/1916.

orchards, where they were stopped by intense machine gun fire. The 10/Royal Fusiliers (111 Brigade) were in support and, in spite of being held up by wounded and sheltering troops in the sunken region of the track, managed to get into the orchards, but in turn were beaten back.

A number of battalion headquarters had been established in the Chalk Pit and at about 2.00 p.m. Major-General Ingouville-Williams visited the scene to assess the situation for himself. Satisfied that no further progress was immediately possible, he arranged for a further bombardment which began at 5.00 p.m. followed by a fresh assault. When this attack went in at 6.00 p.m. the German machine gunners again emerged unscathed from their dugouts and cellars and took a heavy toll. The advance made some ground and the position, when consolidated, ran for about half a mile west-south-west from a point on the Albert-Bapaume road about 300 yards short of Pozières.

Of the bombardment of Pozières the Divisional History records:

> 'Our Battery Commander, from his observation post in Kinfauns, records: July 15th Saturday. Heavy fighting in

The Chalk Pit near Pozières. Past this ran the main track for communication with the front line before and during the battle. The track can be seen on the left of the picture. The photograph was taken at a late stage of the fighting, 28th August, 1916.

Pozières all day. This was the biggest bombardment of it, by all our heavies, I have ever seen. The whole place went up in brick dust, and when it was over no trace of a building could be seen anywhere. It was a wonderful sight, huge clouds of rose-coloured, brown, bluish black and white smoke rolling along together with flashes of bursts, the whole against a pale green blue sky and bright evening sunlight.'

112 Brigade Casualties. 1034.   161 killed and 873 wounded
10/Royal Fusiliers Casualties. 42 Killed, 183 wounded and 24 missing.

The division was relieved by the 1st Australian Division on 19 and 20 July.

The Reserve Army

When Sir Douglas Haig took over from Sir John French in December 1915, one of his first tasks was to plan for a breakthrough in Belgium. At the same time he contemplated the creation of a fifth army to exploit the gap so created by a rapid cavalry pursuit. On 22 May 1916 the

Reserve Army 'Flying Fox'

Reserve Army came into being, and General Sir Hubert Gough was appointed G.O.C. Subsquently it would become the Fifth Army but, since it was not so designated until 30 October 1916, it will be referred to as the Reserve Army for the purposes of this narrative. It was established at Regnière Ecluse, five miles west-north-west of Crécy en Ponthieu, but three weeks later moved to Daours, six miles east of Amiens. On 2 July it was installed at Toutencourt ten miles south-east of Doullens.

As originally planned, its role in the Battle of the Somme was to be one of exploitation and containment. Once the break had been achieved by the Fourth Army Gough was to move forward on both sides of Albert, seize Bapaume, drive off the enemy's counter-attacks, and cover the Fourth Army from the east. Accordingly on 22 June it was allocated three cavalry divisions, followed on 29 June by the 19th and 49th Infantry Divisions. The failures of 1 July necessitated a change of plan and on the evening of that day Gough received fresh orders. He was to take command of two corps which had suffered badly on the left wing of Sir Henry Rawlinson's Fourth Army, X and VIII Corps. He was to reorganise them and continue the attack whilst Rawlinson exploited the success on the right. Once he had visited and interviewed the two corps commanders and reviewed their joint losses, in excess of 20,000 men, he was convinced that neither was in a state to continue the attack next day. He immediately cancelled the attack

General Sir Hubert Gough.

and set to work to reorganise the troops and their positions. As he has recorded:

'I was now faced with an unenviable task. The change was complete; in one day my thoughts and ideas had to move from consolidation of a victorious pursuit to those of the rehabilitation of the shattered wing of an army'[1].

Sir Douglas Haig's new instructions were that for the moment the Reserve Army should not undertake any major operation but would establish itself on the left of the Fourth Army from La Boisselle to Hèbuterne, a front of eight miles, and engage in trench-warfare tactics e.g. sapping, raiding, bombing etc. By 4 July the first objective for the Reserve Army became the capture of Ovillers, which required an extension of the right to included the positions occupied by the 12th Division. The Reserve Army now contained nine divisions: X Corps, 12th 25th 32nd 36th 49th; VIII Corps, 4th 29th 35th 48th. Of these only the 25th, 35th and 48th had not suffered heavily since 1 July.

On 7 July, in heavy rain, which hampered movements by producing thick glutinous mud, the 12th Division renewed the offensive on Ovillers. Zero hour was 8 a.m. for 74 Brigade attacking across the Albert-Bapaume road from La Boisselle and 8.30 a.m. for 36 Brigade, which was positioned in hollow ground to the left of the road running from Ovillers towards Albert. The time difference was intended to permit 74 Brigade to capture the machine guns in Mash Valley, which had wrought so much havoc to troops attacking Ovillers from the direction of 36 Brigade's assault in previous attacks.

The preliminary bombardment opened up at 4.45 a.m. with gas followed, at 6.45 a.m., by heavy artillery and mortars. When 74 Brigade attacked they made some progress but failed in the primary objective of taking out the machine guns. At 8.30 a.m. 36 Brigade went over with three battalions; on the right the 8/Royal Fusiliers, in the centre the 7/Royal Sussex and on the left the 9/Royal Fusiliers. The 11/Middlesex were in reserve. As soon as the 8/Royal Fusiliers left their trenches they lost heavily at the hands of the machine guns in

Mash Valley. As stated in the 12th Division History:

> *'With the third line was the Commanding Officer, Lieutenant-Colonel A. C. Anneseley, who seeing the confusion arising from the heavy casualties, took personal command, and waving his stick in the air shouted the familiar words of a field day, and led the men on. He was wounded in the hand and leg, but continued leading to the enemy's front line where he was hit in the thigh. Shortly afterwards he fell, being hit for the fourth time, shot through the heart. His gallant conduct infected his battalion, and the fourth line coming up, the second and third objectives were carried'* [2].

The History also records that:

> *'during the bombardment of the trenches previous to the assault, and whilst crossing the German trenches, Private F. Warren played his mouth-organ to cheer on his comrades'.*

Lieutenant-Colonel Annesely is buried in Warloy-Baillon Communal Cemetery Extension.

The 7/Royal Sussex gained all three and the 9/Royal Fusiliers the first and second objectives but, such were the conditions, all communications with brigade headquarters was impossible. At midday Lieutenant-Colonel W.L. Osborn commanding the 7/Royal Sussex took overall command and withdrew both 7/Royal Sussex and the 8/Royal Fusiliers to a position in their first and second objectives.

74 Brigade made no headway so at 11.30 a.m., the 7/Suffolk Regiment was sent as reinforcement to La Boisselle whilst at 5 p.m. the 7/East Surrey and 9/Essex Regiments were sent to 36 Brigade. By evening more definite reports of the situation in Ovillers were being received and the East Surrey and Essex Regiments were sent forward to consolidate the line held by 36 Brigade. As no contact had been achieved between the two brigades, 35 Brigade was ordered to take the German trenches between the two and so bridge the gap. This order was carried out on 8 July. During the remainder of the 8th further progress was made through the village which brought the division to the summit of the spur on which the village stood, with good views towards Pozières. Ovillers was finally cleared of the enemy by the 48th Division between 5 and 17 July.

On 11 July Rawlinson told Haig that the successful continuation of the offensive was being seriously jeopardized by the stubborn resistance of the Germans in and around the village of Pozières. He emphasised that in his opinion, "Pozières was the key to the area". In the plans for the attack of 14 July the Fourth Army south of the Albert-

Bapaume road was ordered to press forward from Contalmaison to Contalmaison Villa and in the direction of Pozières, whilst the Reserve Army was merely to keep in touch with its left flank. In the event the centre and right flanks, XV and XIII Corps, gained considerable ground but on the left III Corps was stopped short. This resulted in a salient between Bazentin le Petit and Delville Wood in the direction of High Wood which was open to German counter-attack.

As explained in *Sir Douglas Haig's Command* by Dewar and Boraston

> *'there were two courses open to the British Command - it would have been possible to have formed on the British right a defensive flank resting on the Combles valley, and to have developed our principal attack northwards. To have adopted this plan would have meant abandoning the idea of continuing the offensive as a joint operation in close association with the French. On the other hand, the closing of the German attacks at Verdun would give many French divisions time to rest and refit - it followed that in due course the French should be in a position to take a more important share in the Somme battle. These considerations decided the British Commander-in-Chief to turn away from the attractive scheme of a British attack northwards, and to devote his main efforts to gaining ground to the east, in co-operation with the French. Accordingly, the boundary between the Fourth and Reserve Armies was adjusted, and further operations against Pozières were handed to General Gough '[3].*

In consequence of this decision, Haig allotted I Anzac[4], consisting of the 1st, 2nd and 4th Australian Divisions, to the Reserve Army on 17 July.

Bibliography
1. *The Fifth Army.* General Sir Hubert Gough. Hodder & Stoughton 1931.
2. *History of the 12th Division in the Great War.* Scott & Brumwell. Nisbet. 1923.
3. *Sir Douglas Haig's Command 1915-1918.* Dewar & Boraston. Constable 1922.
4. **A**ustralian **N**ew **Z**ealand **A**rmy Corps.

Chapter Two

THE AUSTRALIANS ON THE SOMME I

Pozières

I Anzac consisted of the 1st, 2nd and 4th Australian Divisions. It was brought into the Somme area from service with the Second Army in northern France where its experience of conditions on the Western Front was limited to about three months in trenches around Armentières. Its commander Lieutenant-General Sir William Birdwood, set up his headquarters in Vignacourt on the morning of 10 July whilst the three divisions began to take up billets in other villages around Amiens. By the start of the 14 July offensive they had been moved closer to Albert and, given the greater accessibility of the Corps to the combat areas and the successes on the 14th, expectation was high that the Corps would be allocated to the Fourth Army to exploit those successes. Instead, as already noted, Sir Douglas Haig opted to use the Reserve Army to take Pozières and to utilise the 1 Anzac and in particular the 1st Division. The Division, commanded by Lieutenant-General Sir H. B. Walker, was already in the area, located around Contay and Warloy-Baillon - 12 miles from the action. General Gough, instructed by Haig to take Pozières with as little delay as possible, opted to carry out the attack using Reserve Army staff rather than to await the arrival of the Anzac staff. General Walker was, not unexpectedly, unhappy about this suggestion but pushed on with arrangements to get the Division into the line south of Pozières. He set up his headquarters in Albert and after visiting the battle area decided to attack from the south-east on a front of one mile. The trenches

Australian transport behind the line. TAYLOR LIBRARY

MAP 5. Trench Map Pozières defence system.

Pozières

Dvillers-
Boisselle

Contalmaison
Wood

Chalk Pit

Bailiff Wood

Chateau

Cemetery

Spring Gardens

Centre Way

Smythe Valley

Howitzer Av

This view
taken on 28
August, 1916,
from the
Centre Way,
near where it
ran into
O.G.1. On the
right is seen a
heap of spoil,
marking one
of the
German
dugouts in
O.G.1.

TAYLOR LIBRARY

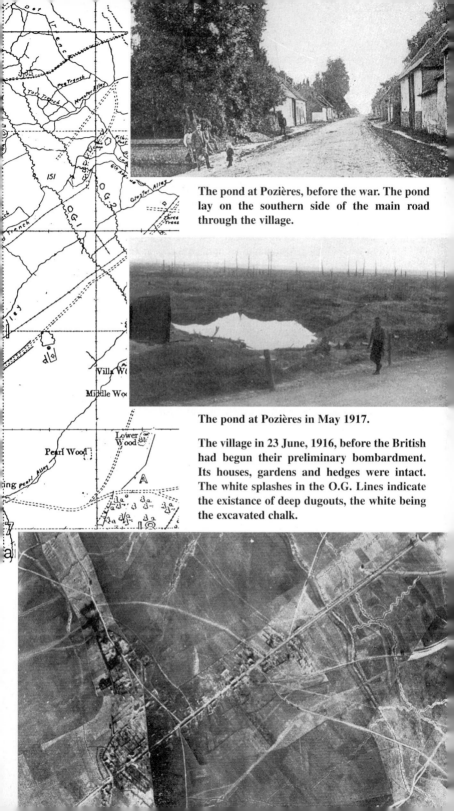

The pond at Pozières, before the war. The pond lay on the southern side of the main road through the village.

The pond at Pozières in May 1917.

The village in 23 June, 1916, before the British had begun their preliminary bombardment. Its houses, gardens and hedges were intact. The white splashes in the O.G. Lines indicate the existance of deep dugouts, the white being the excavated chalk.

around Pozières are shown on **map 5**, which is a modified trench map dated 1 September 1916. At the time of the Australians' entry into the battle many of the trenches shown existed, but not all the names given were allocated or in use. Some of the trenches were also known by two names. Western Trench, which ran along the western side of the village, was more commonly known as K Trench. Ration Trench and Skyline Trench were known as 5th Avenue and 6th Avenue respectively. The two major trenches of the German second line were known as OG 1 and OG 2 and the two together referred to as the OG Lines. **Map 5** should be used in conjunction with subsequent maps giving positions for particular actions.

The attack was to be carried out by two brigades, 1 and 3 with 2 in reserve. 3 Brigade on the right would attack part of Pozières Trench and part of the OG Lines whilst 1 Brigade on the left would concentrate on Pozières Trench. On the night of 19/20 July the Australians took over the British line in front of Pozières. Leaving Albert, 3 Brigade made its way over Tara Hill and on to Avoca Valley, over Chape's Spur and into Sausage Valley following the route of a trench railway line, which ran up to Gordon Dump, the new name for Gordon Post established by the 34th Division. At the head of Sausage Valley they turned right into the relative safety of the sunken road running down to Contalmaison from La Boisselle. Here they joined the route taken by 1 Brigade which had marched to La Boisselle before leaving the Albert-Bapaume road. After about 500 yards they arrived at a cross roads - Casualty Corner. 1 Brigade, destined for the line south-west of Pozières, turned left here on to a track running up to the village. On their left, in the angle between this track and the

The line of K Trench behind Pozières villiage from village cemetery.

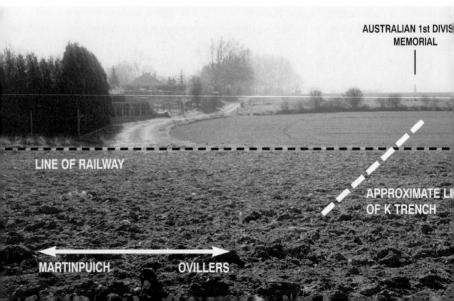

AUSTRALIAN 1st DIVIS
MEMORIAL

LINE OF RAILWAY

APPROXIMATE LI
OF K TRENCH

MARTINPUICH   OVILLERS

Round the field kitchen. Sausage Valley, taken on 26 May 1917. TAYLOR LIBRARY

Contalmaison road, had been established an aid-post, hence the name, Casualty Corner. This track gave some protection as they made their way up past the Chalk Pit - scene of Ingouville-Williams' visit to the battlefield on 15 July - and entered new trenches emanating from the sunken road at the northern end of the track. This stretch of track was later to be known as Dead Man's Road or Smyth Valley. 3 Brigade continued along the Contalmaison road to enter the south-eastern side of the line using what was originally a German communication trench - Black Watch Alley - so named as it had recently been captured by the 1st Battalion, the Black Watch, 1 Brigade, 1st Division. From Black Watch Alley the brigade moved forward into as yet incomplete 'jumping off' trenches. Operation Order No 19 [1] issued by the Reserve Army 18 July stated that the Australians would be able to take over part of OG 1 and a section of Pozières Trench between OG 1 and a point about 250 yards along it in a westerly direction. This proved to be incorrect as the British 1st Division had been mistaken in its reported position. To rectify the mistake, on 18 July the 2/Royal Munster Fusiliers, 3 Brigade 1st Division, attempted to take some 800 yards of

Sausage Valley looking towards Gordon Dump Cemetery from near La Boisselle.

GORDON DUMP CEMETERY

enemy trench in the region of OG 1 and OG 2. The attack was unsuccessful but the Munsters did manage to enter a length of the switch trench which ran back into the German trench system, henceforth known as 'Munster Alley'. In the Reserve Army War Diary entry dated 20 July[2] it is made clear that the Australians had taken over a line running approximately from point X.11.b 9.7 to point X.4.c 5.5[3] during the previous night. It should not be assumed that this relief was carried out without difficulty. The whole area was under incessant heavy and medium artillery bombardment as well as machine gun fire. Lachrimatory and poison gas shells were also used which necessitated prolonged use of respirators.

General Walker was still not satisfied with the preparations, particularly the lack of forward trenches required to reduce the distance to be covered in the open to reach Pozières Trench. He made strong representations to Reserve Army headquarters and in consequence the projected attack was put back from the night of 20 July to that of 21 July. At the same time the objectives were altered, instead of simply attacking Pozières Trench they were to press on to the orchards in front of the village, using the railway track as a guide, and finally to the southern edge of the Albert-Bapaume road, from the orchard, west of the village, to a point in the O G Lines near the mill.

The preliminary bombardment for the attack had started on 19 July

18 Pounder. Battle of Pozières Ridge.

Australian Artillery prepare for the bombardment.

but in support of the modified plan the artillery role at the time of the assault was changed. The new scheme was: two minute bombardment of Pozières Trench and OG Lines prior to attack; thirty minute bombardment of second objective during initial attack; thirty minute bombardment of third objective during attack on second objective; barrage 100 yards north of main road while attack completed.

Late in the afternoon of 21 July the attack was again postponed, at least partly in response to the need to modify the artillery instructions, until 12.30 a.m. on Sunday 23 July. By so doing it became part of a much larger operation, the left flank of an attack stretching to the right as far as High Wood.

At 12.28 am on 23 July the final phase of the bombardment started. The whole area around Pozières was blasted by artillery from a number of divisions. The 25th Division concentrated on Western Trench, 1st Australian Division on Pozières Trench while 34th Division, 48th Division and some French units covered remaining areas. A particularly enterprising action was carried out by Lieutenant Samuel. R. Thurnhill[4] 6 Battery, Australian Field Artillery. Under cover of the existing bombardment, he and his team manoeuvred his gun into a position on the Albert-Bapaume road about 400 yards from the village, quite close to the point where the track from Casualty Corner joined

Approximate position of Lieutenant S Thurnhill's gun, 23 July 1916.

the main road. From here he was able to fire in excess of 100 rounds directly into the village.

When this intensified bombardment started the Germans immediately laid down a counter barrage which, although not badly affecting the troops of the initial assaulting battalions, caught those of the second line moving up from Albert. Bean describes the scene on their way up:

> 'the road past Casualty Corner to Contalmaison was intermittently swept with shrapnel and high-explosive, and drenched with phosgene gas shell. At times the corner could only be passed by men running one at a time; those who were hit had to crawl away from the place as best they could, their mates having at that moment one paramount duty to reach their starting point for the attack'[5]

1 Brigade, on the left, was to attack with four Battalions each in two waves. The first and second objectives were to be taken by, from left to right, the 2nd and 1st Battalions and the third by the 4th and 3rd Battalions passing through the 2nd and 1st respectively. Similarly 3 Brigade, on the right, was to employ the 11th and 9th Battalions

Cross-road leading to Casualty Corner. Through this road went the traffic to Pozières. Casualty Corner is out of sight behind the nearer hill. In the distance is Contalmaison being shelled by the Germans. High Wood is on the left in the distance, which was still held by the Germans at the date of this photograph.

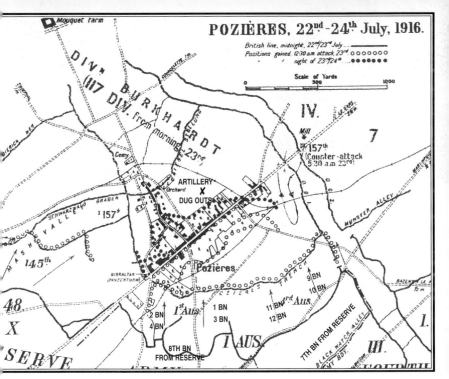

Map 6. Pozières, 22-24 July 1916. (Based on Official History Map).

followed by the 12th and 10th **(See map 6)**.

At 12.30 a.m., exactly according to plan, the assault went in. Such had been the ferocity and length of the bombardment that it was difficult for the Australians to distinguish formal trenches from the multitude of shell holes and small craters. As the first waves moved out from positions, often in front of the formal starting trenches, little resistance was encountered. The first objectives were taken and the following waves were able to pass through ready to continue the attack. On the extreme right in the vicinity of OG 1 and OG 2 the success was more limited and a series of bloody actions ensued. Following the

The road from La Boisselle to Contalmaison at Casualty Corner.

Drawing water for the guns' crews. Working a heavy gun is thirsty work.

earlier failures to extend the grip on the double line of trenches, the 9th Battalion decided to attack in a line moving up through the ground between the OG Lines. Owing to intense enemy fire they were forced to split into left and right hand parties. Troops on the left passed the junction of OG 1 with Pozières Trench, which was unoccupied, but were soon held up by a combination of machine gun fire and bombs emanating from a strong point in OG 1 at its junction with a communication trench leading to Munster Alley. Before orders could be given to overcome this hold up, Private John Leak ran forward, bombed the German position and then jumped into the strong point to complete its capture by use of the bayonet. Shortly afterwards, when the officer in charge, Lieutenant C. Monteath, entered the point, he found Leak wiping blood off his bayonet with his felt hat. For this heroic deed Leak was awarded the Victoria Cross.

It was, however, soon clear to Monteath that without fresh supplies of bombs and reinforcements his hold on OG 1 was not sustainable. At 1.30 a.m. an attempt to relieve Monteath was carried out by a party of the 10th Battalion under Captain W. McCann. As they moved up OG 1 they met men of the 9th Battalion who had been driven back by a German counter attack, but managed to reach the junction of OG 1 with Pozières Trench, now occupied and blocked by barricade. Here they came under intense machine gun fire from a point later found to be in the communication trench running form OG 1 to Munster Alley, which forced them to withdraw to a position 120 yards back down OG 1. As dawn broke, McCann, who had been seriously wounded, was joined by Lieutenant A. Blackburn, who was about to win the second Victoria Cross awarded to an Australian at Pozières. Blackburn had been sent forward with 50 men and two teams of bombers in an attempt to complete the capture of OG 1. He quickly gained a further 100 yards of the trench but was then stopped by machine gun fire from both OG 2 and the strong point in the communication trench. Even after the point had been subjected to a mortar attack, the machine gun continued to fire, making further progress almost impossible. In spite of this Blackburn continued to go forward until he made contact with troops of the 9th Battalion in Pozières Trench, via a tunnel where OG 1 ran under what remained of the road from Pozières to Bazentin le Petit. He then made repeated attempts to capture the enemy strong point until ordered to hold on where he was. It was for his persistence that he was awarded the Victoria Cross. Thus, only the first objective was gained in OG 1. The right hand party under Lieutenant N. Armstrong moved forward but, on reaching the position where they believed the enemy trench to be, could not identify it due to the state of the ground. They lost their bearings, eventually managing to struggle back to their own line. Further attempts to locate the trench also failed and the strong point remained in enemy hands until 25 July. However, the link up with men in Pozières Trench meant that the whole of the first objective was secure. When the two brigades moved forward to the second and third objectives they were subjected to enfilade fire from the right flank. Nevertheless by 2.30 a.m. a new front line was being constructed along the edge of the Albert-Bapaume road, but instead of reaching beyond OG 2 it bent back to form a depressed flank towards the junction of Pozières Trench and OG 1. Such had been the enthusiasm of the Australians to advance that the later waves, who were provided with picks and shovels to dig the new lines, discarded what they considered to be 'superfluous equipment'. They were to regret this when they were forced to dig the new line with entrenching tools.

One officer to be killed in the attack was Lieutenant Walter Host MM of the 2nd Battalion. An account of his death was given by his friend Captain Ken Millar.

> *The night before the attack, Host and O'Connell made a daring patrol, and found that they could occupy an advanced German trench for the hop-over. We attacked successfully. Host and I had a working arrangement to link up. Just on daylight he heard I was wounded and still in the trench, so he came along just about the time Rowlands had reached me. They fixed me up and eventually I was carried away. Neither Rowlands nor Host was concerned about his own safety, but only about my wounds. I wished them good luck, and watched Host, smiling, walk away*

Artists impression of the taking of Pozières. NATIONAL ARMY MUSEUM

back to his men, the pride of old D company. That morning he
had the time of his life wandering around collecting prisoners.
One drew an automatic pistol and shot him in the stomach. He
died at the dressing station and was buried in Warloy Cemetery'.[6]

On the evening of the 23rd General Haig gave instructions for units to
continue the offensive with localised rather than general attacks. As
part of this strategy the Australian and British 1st Divisions were to co-
operate in capturing the OG Lines, and in particular the strong point at
the junction of OG 2 and Munster Alley, using direct attack rather than
the hitherto unsuccessful 'bombing up' technique. In the event no
attack took place until much later.

Reports received during the 23rd indicated that the Germans had all
but evacuated the village, leaving only isolated groups of snipers, but
that they still occupied K Trench in strength. Gough ordered that the
bombardment of K Trench was to be maintained but that on the village
itself should be stopped to permit the Australians to advance across the
road and into the village proper. However, during the day before action
could be taken on Gough's directive, the 2nd Battalion, on the left, had
moved to investigate a large concrete structure beyond the village at
the junction with K Trench. Here they captured three officers and
twenty three men in what turned out to be a large fortified observation
and machine gun post. As the village was still subject to the barrage
they withdrew back across the road. When at 5 p.m. the barrage lifted
they quickly moved back to occupy what they christened Gibraltar. The
German name was Panzerturm, meaning armoured turret. They set

about incorporating it into their forward line and at the same time bombed up the southern most part of K Trench before erecting a barrier. The 8th Battalion, which had been allocated to 1 Brigade from the reserve 2 Brigade, entered the village at about 11 p.m. and went steadily northwards to a point mid-way between the ruined church and the orchard when disaster struck. The officer in charge, Captain George James[7] was mortally wounded by Australian machine gun fire from the rear. They then dug in, leaving the remainder of the village unoccupied. Further east the 11th Battalion sent out patrols during the day but were held up by fire from the artillery dug-outs and forced to retire. On the extreme right patrols from the 12th Battalion, aided by the 11th, went out just as dusk was falling. They entered and incorporated an old German trench system along the railway line, henceforth known as Tramway Trench. Whilst so engaged they discovered a deep dug-out, afterwards known as Medical Dugout. From this dug-out a number of Germans emerged including an officer, Captain Ponsonby Lyons, the commandant of Pozières, whose grandfather had been English. With problems in communication, no further advance was instituted nor was progress made in the region of

Carrying party of the 7th Brigade passing 'Gibraltar'. The photograph shows the fortified entrance to a well know head-quarters dugout in Pozières, on 28th August, 1916. No trace remained of the house which once stood here, but the cellar stairway had been fortified and its concrete covering is indicated by the slope to the right of the entrance. From the cellar some twenty steps led down to a still deeper chamber excavated by the Germans. IWM Q1089

OG 1 or OG 2. Although the Australians now had a firm grip on Pozières village, a gap existed between the 8th and 12th Battalions across its centre and the Germans still held the majority of K Trench, a major section of the OG Lines and the Artillery Dugouts, although the latter were relinquished the next day.

23 July was summed up in the History of the 1st Battalion of the A.I.F.

> 'Sunday passed comparatively quietly. The line was not shelled very much, and we spent the day consolidating the positions taken up in the attack. Much hard work was done, none of us dreaming of the hell that was soon to burst upon us'[8].

On 24 July Gough again urged the Anzacs to complete the capture of Pozières, drive forward to Mouquet Farm and thereby complete the cutting off of Thiepval. Two linked operations were planned for the night of 24/25 July; an assault on the OG Lines at 2 a.m. followed by an advance through the village at 3.30 a.m.

As preparations for the double attack were made during the 24th the German barrage tactics changed. Hitherto the focal point had been the rear area, now it became the Australian front line and in particular the line of the main road, the track up past the Chalk Pit and the junction of that track with the main road. The attack on the OG Lines was carried out by the 5th Battalion with two companies of the 7th **(See maps 6 and 7)**. The plan required a manoeuvre to be carried out in the dark and under enemy fire which would have been difficult enough on a parade ground. The attackers had to leave Black Watch Alley, cross over Pozières Trench and then turn left to face the enemy in OG 1. Needless to say things went wrong. Of the two companies of the 7th who were to attack between the road and the railway track, one lost its

The dug out where the commandant of Pozières surrendered. IWM E(AUS) 992

bearing and turned towards the village and took no part in the attack. The other made no progress, being driven back before it even reached OG 1. The 5th Battalion entered OG 1 and then passed on to OG 2 and at the same time a bombing party of the 10th attacked and over ran the strong point in the communication trench between OG 1 and Munster Alley. As the Australians surveyed the remnants of OG 2 they were surprised to see Germans moving along OG 1 from the direction of the main road and flares rising from Munster Alley. To avoid being cut off they withdrew to OG 1 where a desperate bomb-fight ensued. After several hours the Germans fell back, leaving the Australians in control of OG 1 about half way to the railway, where a barricade was set up, and of the communication trench between OG 1 and Munster Alley.

The second part of the dual operation was also experiencing problems. As part of a plan to link the village with the OG Lines, the 12th Battalion had been detailed to organise a strong point at the eastern end of the village in the junction of the main road and the road on the left up to Courcelette. The 11th Battalion, in preparation for the attack at 3.30 a.m., moved forward and occupied the artillery dug-outs which had been abandoned by the Germans, but then came under fire from their left. The dug-outs had also been attacked by the right flank of the 8th Battalion and it was not until daylight that the problem was sorted out and the dug-outs handed over to the 8th. The remainder of the 8th moved forward at 3.55 a.m. a little behind schedule, together with the 4th Battalion bombing up K Trench. The two units met up about 50 yards beyond the cemetery when, by crossing into K Trench, the 8th trapped a number of the enemy between themselves and the 4th. These Germans made good their escape by climbing out of the trench and running either towards the OG Lines or westward into trenches beyond K. Gough's orders had stated that the advance must take in the junctions of K Trench with Third Avenue (Schwarzwaldgraben) and with Fourth Avenue (Ganter Weg). This was not completed until 4 a.m. on the 26th when the 7/Warwicks linked up with the Australians in Fourth Avenue, having gained Third Avenue at dusk the previous evening. It was in this action of the 8th Battalion that Private Cooke was awarded the Victoria Cross.

During the day the German barrage continued with a ferocity hitherto unknown. Colonel C. Elliot of the 12th Battalion is quoted in The Story of the 12th:

'Later we experienced many hurricane bombardments, lasting half-an-hour or more, of far greater intensity, but I do not remember any other so severe for such a long time ....in the *evening when I went to arrange for our relief by the 19th Battalion, I could hardly find a trace of the trenches that had been so well dug the previous day'.*[9]

Such was the bombardment that it was suspected that it must be a precursor to a counter-attack. A particularly vulnerable point would have been the position gained in OG 1. In their suspicions the Australians were correct but the attack planned for 4.30 p.m. was cancelled only one hour before launch by General von Boehm. He had concluded that to retake Pozières would be too costly in both men and material.

When at last the bombardment eased, so the time had come for the relief of 1 and 3 Brigades, which commenced on the evening of 25 July and was completed by early morning of 26 July.

Of the battalions of 2 Brigade the 6th and 8th were already in the line, and the 7th replaced the 1st and 2nd Battalions in support positions in K Trench and along the main road. Of 5 Brigade (2nd Australian Division) the 17th Battalion relieved the 9th Battalion in the OG Lines and the 19th Battalion relieved the 12th Battalion east of the village, the 18th Battalion replaced the 10th Battalion leaving the 20th Battalion in reserve.

There remained one area where no progress had been made, that

Map 7. Pozières, 25 July 1916. (Based on Official History Map).

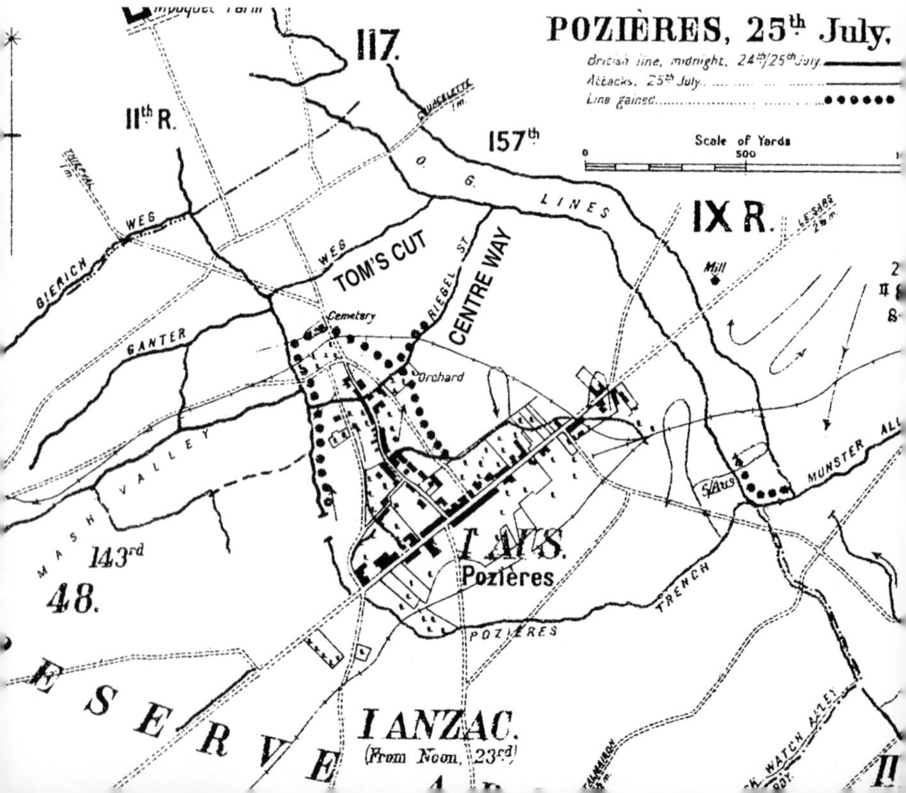

being the region between the OG Lines and the western edge of the village. Just before daylight on 26 July a party of the 8th Battalion crawled out into No Man's Land and dug themselves in on either side of what was to be known as Centre Way. Just after dark in the evening of the same day they completed a similar task in what became known as Tom's Cut. At 7 a.m. on the 26th the Germans unleashed another bombardment comparable with that of the 25th which, with only short breaks, was to last all day. Bean states that:

> 'the village constantly hidden in rolling clouds of dust and smoke, was again the spectacle of the battlefield'[10].

The density of the cloud over the battlefield hampered attempts by the Australian and British artillery to locate and destroy the German batteries that were pounding Pozières. So debilitating was the bombardment that during the night of 26/27 July the remnants of the Australian 1st Division were replaced by two battalions of the Australian 2nd Division.

During their time in the line at Pozières the Australian 1st Division lost 181 officers and over 5000 other ranks.

As the Australian 2nd Division entered the battle, orders were received for the Anzacs to continue northwards whilst II Corps extended its attack on the area to the west of K Trench. On the 27th, staff of the 2nd Division issued an order maintaining the artillery bombardment of enemy lines in preparation for an attack the exact time and date of which would be decided by Major-General J. Legge. Both of the brigades already in the line were under pressure. 5 had been engaged in a struggle for Munster Alley when they assisted an attack by the British 1st Division on 26th July and 6 had been under constant artillery bombardment but, even in such horrendous conditions, could turn their minds to other things. Bean quotes the 24th Battalion History:

> 'an officer passing along K Trench saw four men playing cards. On the parapet above them was the body of their sergeant who had been playing with them, his hand when he was killed, being taken by a mate. When the officer passed that way again, those four men were dead'. [11]

Under pressure from Gough, Legge proposed to attack on the night of 28/29 July even though he was not in a position to carry out two very necessary preparatory operations. As already noted, the smoke and dust created by the bombardments obscured observation, so there was no way he could ascertain whether the two large belts of wire in front of and between OG 1 and OG 2 had been destroyed. Nor could

Wounded from the battle of Pozières Ridge.

suitable 'jumping off' trenches be dug within two hundred yards of the first objective. All that could be achieved in the time available was to extend Tramway Trench into the area between the village and OG 1, sometimes only as a line of shell holes, and to dig a third strong point between the trench and OG 1.

The main assaulting force was to be 7 Brigade, from Tramway Trench **(See map 8)**, which was brought forward from Albert on the evening of the 28th. Their objective was the OG Lines from the Ovillers-Courcelette track to the main road, using three battalions, from left to right 26th, 25th and 28th with the 27th in reserve. On either side, 6 Brigade was to attack the Ovillers-Courcelette track north of Pozières, taking Tom's Cut on the way whilst to the south-east two companies of the 20th battalion would attack the OGs between the main road and the railway and then move down OG 2 to meet bombers from the 17th coming up.

The attack was set for 12.15 a.m. following a three minute intense barrage which would pass to OG 2 for a further 10 minutes before lifting to concentrate on areas behind the OGs. For several hours the success or failure of the attack was unclear but at 3.15 a.m. definite, if mainly bad, news was obtained. 6 Brigade had carried all their objectives and were digging in along the line of the Ovillers-Courcelette track but the other two assaults had failed. 7 had, in part, reached OG 2 but had then been driven back while some of the brigade had been held up and trapped on uncut wire. To the south the two companies of the 20th had been cut down even as they began to move forward and in consequence the bombing party had not left their starting positions.

The first major offensive carried out by the Australian 2nd Division was almost a total failure. The losses incurred by the division were 3500 since entering the line. Gough has been the subject of much criticism for insisting that Legge attack before thorough preparations

Map 8. Pozières, 26-29 July 1916. (Based on Official History Map).

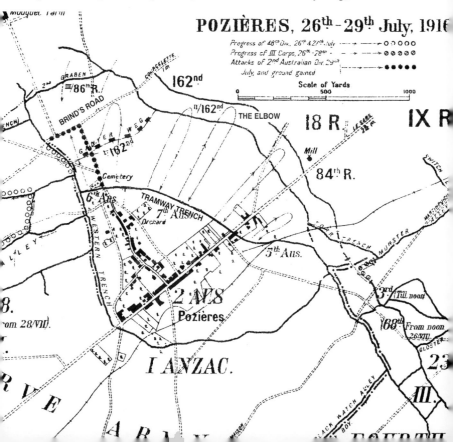

had been completed. Both Legge and his staff lacked experience of fighting and directing operations under conditions prevailing at Pozières. The attack on 23 July had been delayed until it became part of a large operation but no such large operation was planned for the near future. So why not wait a few days to prepare adequate jumping off trenches and complete other preliminaries? An isolated and limited attack was always easier for the enemy to contain and it is arguable that Gough should have staid the hand of Legge rather than forcing him to attack when ill prepared. The loss of life which resulted was seen by the Australians as unnecessary and the fault of bad British leadership. It was to become a source of resentment and bitterness which has continued even to this day.

Haig, in his diary entry for 29 July, wrote:

'The attack by the 2nd Australian Division upon the enemy's position between Pozières and the Windmill was not successful last night. From several reports, I think the cause was due to want of thorough preparation.

After lunch, I visited H.Q. Reserve Army and impressed on Gough and his G.S.O. (Neil Malcolm) that they must supervise more closely the plans of the Anzac Corps. Some of their Divisional Generals are so ignorant and (like many Colonials) so conceited, that they cannot be trusted to work out unaided the plans of attack'[12].

In spite of the terrible losses the division wished to continue and, following a hastily convened conference on 29 July, an order was drawn up for the attack to be repeated on the night of 30/31 July. With help from General Sir C.B.White, Birdwood's Chief of Staff and a noted tactician, Legge set about preparing for the new attack but in a much more thorough way. The 2nd Division artillery replaced that of the 1st Division, which had done sterling work for over two weeks. The new Corps Artillery Commander Major-General W. Napier informed Legge that to ensure complete destruction of the protective wire and the trenches of the OG Lines, bombardment with heavy howitzers was necessary and could be achieved by delivery of in excess of 5000 shells prior to the attack. The attack was set for 9.15 p.m. to give the troops sufficient light to see their objectives but resulted in the jumping off trenches being visible to the enemy. Therefore not only the jumping off trenches had to be dug but communication ones as well. As work progressed the date for the assault was put back but Legge hoped to be ready by 3 August; White, at Corps headquarters, considering this to be over optimistic contacted Gough, who was, as ever, eager to press forward, ordered Legge to wait until the evening of Friday 4 August. By then the system of jumping off trenches with communication trenches running back south of the main road would be completed.

At 6 p.m. the final stage of the bombardment commenced, but utilising a programme which had been followed for several days, so as not to alert the Germans to the imminence of an attack. At 9.00 p.m. the barrage stopped, but at 9.15 p.m. both heavy and field guns resumed firing on OG 1 and after three minutes both lifted to OG 2 for a further three minutes before lifting to areas to the rear of the enemy lines. 5 Brigade, south of the main road, quickly took OG 1, entering the line before the defenders could get up out of their dugouts and the successive waves passed through to capture OG 2 which they, in common with other units in the attack, had difficulty in identifying, relying for recognition on the line of stakes which had carried the defensive belts of wire. 7 Brigade on their left, in Tramway Trench, fared almost as well, but suffered some confusion when the leading waves found that, contrary to reports, jumping off trenches on the 26th Battalion front were incomplete. They used those of the 25th which led to a build up of troops moving up, the fourth wave caught in the enemy counter fire lost their commanding officer, Major Trevor Cunningham.[13] In spite of these difficulties the leading waves of the 26th Battalion captured OG 1 with ease and themselves passed on to OG 2. Similarly the 25th battalion captured OG 1 and OG 2 north-west of the Elbow, unfortunately the 27th Battalion who were to carry the OG Lines from the Elbow to the main road, advanced too far and ran into their own barrage. On retiring the survivors found that no support was available and so retired to hold OG 1 where they were helped by the arrival of Lieutenant P.H. Cherry [14] of the 26th Battalion with four machine guns and set up a defensive line.

Further north the 22nd Battalion experienced problems getting to

General view of the battlefield near Pozières 20 September 1916. IWM Q1090

the jumping off trenches due to an organisational mistake allocating two units to the same communication trenches. In the moment of crisis Major M. Mackay ordered his men out into the open to by-pass the hold up and so gain their starting positions. Here they caught up with the leading companies who had passed the problem point before the two units met. The delays meant that their assault did not take place until 9.40 p.m. by which time a German machine gun had been set up on the Ovillers-Courcelette track (Brind's Road). It took heavy toll of the 22nd Battalion, including Major Mackay, but the survivors captured both objectives. To link up the left flank in OG 1 and OG 2 with the corresponding position in K Trench a party of the 23rd Battalion was sent out to dig in along the line of the Ovillers-Courcelette track but were also caught in the fire from the machine gun that had already done so much damage to the 22nd Battalion. Although they managed to reach the vicinity of OG 1 a strong flank position was not established until the following day when the machine gun was finally located and captured. By nightfall the whole objective had been taken, with the exception of the length of OG 2 in front of the 27th Battalion.

As soon as the attack was perceived the enemy laid down a counter barrage on the Australian front line, Tramway Trench, which continued until midnight when it was brought back to fall on the OG Lines. Both barrages had the effect of hindering the consolidation and digging of communication trenches necessary to establish a firm hold on the ground captured. At about 4.00 a.m. a line of enemy soldiers was seen approaching north and south of the Elbow but were soon stopped by machine gun and rifle fire. Reinforcements in the form of two companies of the 28th Battalion under Captain C.M. Fosse were sent forward in the 27th Battalion area, whereupon the Germans being heavily outnumbered surrendered. Fosse led his men on to capture the ground around the ruin of the windmill and so completed the taking of the objectives.

During 6 August much activity was observed in the German areas and, together with the continued heavy bombardment and the presence of three observation balloons, was taken by Lieutenant-Colonel R. Leane Commanding Officer 48th Battalion to be indicative of the proximity of a counter-attack, probably during the next night. At dusk 7 Brigade troops north of the Elbow were at last relieved by the 14th Battalion of 4 Brigade. The OG Lines were then held by comparatively fresh troops but OG 2 in the region between the Elbow and the windmill was only garrisoned by Lewis gunners, leaving the main defenders in OG 1. As the night progressed the bombardment, although concentrated on the OG Lines, also encompassed all the back areas. At dawn there occurred what Bean has described

'as the most dramatic and effective act of individual audacity in the history of the AIF'. [15]

Lieutenant Albert Jacka VC, the first Australian to be so decorated, was in a dug-out in OG 1 in the vicinity of the Elbow, the southernmost unit of the 14th Battalion. On his left was Lieutenant H. Dobbie, part of whose platoon was in OG 2. At 4.00 a.m. the enemy barrage lifted on to Pozières and a large number of Germans were seen advancing towards the OG Lines from Courcelette. The line passed just south of the position held by Jacka, who was oblivious to their presence until his dug-out was filled with smoke and debris from a grenade tossed down by the passing Germans. Jacka rushed out into the open air with seven or eight men. The attacking Germans had been fired on by the 15th Battalion further north and by the 48th from the south but the latter battalion had now withdrawn its machine guns from OG 2 back into OG 1 with the exception of Captain D. Twining in a post near the site of the windmill. The left flank of the attack swung southwards, taking the northern flank of the 48th Battalion in the rear, overrunning them and taking about 50 prisoners, who were sent back under escort in the direction of Courcelette. As Jacka emerged he could see the enemy who had passed him by and were moving down the slope from OG 1 towards Pozières. At the same time the column of 48th Battalion prisoners was coming towards him. He and his small group opened fire on the prisoners' guards some of whom retaliated but others threw

Australian machine-gunners returning from the trenches.

down their arms and surrendered. All his party suffered wounds but the action inspired the prisoners to break away, some picking up the jettisoned arms and joining the fight. On seeing what had happened a sergeant of the 48th Battalion rushed out from the safety of a trench to render assistance as did other Australians who, since the fight was on the forward slope, could see what was going on from their trenches and strong points in front of Tramway Trench. It was difficult to use guns as so many Australians were now in the open, so a vicious bayonet to bayonet contest ensued. Some of the Germans were bombers who, taking cover in shell holes, started throwing their bombs but Jacka jumped in upon them killing several before himself being severely wounded As the numbers of Australians in the fight grew so it became apparent to the Germans that resistance was futile and those still alive surrendered. Thus ended the final attempt of the Germans to recapture the Pozières Heights. During the morning mopping up was completed and at 2.30 p.m. the 47th Battalion began to relieve the 48th and the whole front line was reoccupied.

The 2nd Division infantry was removed completely by 7 August. It had been under almost continuous bombardment for twelve days and lost 230 officers and over 6600 other ranks.

Pozières: The German perspective

Before embarking upon a description of the capture of Pozières from the German perspective it may be helpful to give some insight into the structures employed by the German army.

A German division comprised three infantry brigades together with divisional troops. Each infantry brigade was made up of three infantry regiments and each regiment of three battalions, at this stage, which were usually identified by roman numerals I, II and III. Each battalion consisted of four companies identified by Arabic numerals, and a machine gun company. Companies were always numbered 1 to 12 throughout the regiment. Thus I battalion comprised companies 1,2,3 and 4, II battalion companies 5,6,7 and 8 and III battalion companies 9,10,11 and 12. The abbreviations I.R and R.I.R were used to identify an Infantry Regiment and a Reserve Infantry Regiment respectively. Often I.R. was dropped and reserve regiments indicated by R after the numerial.[16]

A composite division, Division Burkhardt, covered the area between Thiepval and the Albert-Bapaume road at Pozières. This division, created after the break up of the 10th Bavarian Division in the early part of July, was made up of the 8th Bavarian Regiment, two

Battalions of 15th Reserve Regiment, the 185th Regiment and one Battalion of 186th Regiment.

To the left of the road, as far as Bazentin le Petit, the 7th Infantry Division held the line. It was made up of the 26th, 27th and 165th Infantry Regiments, all of which had suffered huge numbers of casualties in earlier fighting and had been augmented by loans from other units.

Division Burkhardt had been heavily involved in the defence of Ovillers and so, in order to strengthen the strategic position of the Pozières Ridge, the 117th Division was moved down from Ypres to take over their defensive positions. This division comprised two Reserve Infantry Regiments, the 11th and 22nd and the 157th Infantry Regiment.

On the night of 20 July the 157th started to relieve Division Burkhardt by taking over K Trench (Western Trench) and 1000 yards of Schwarzwaldgraben (Third Avenue) facing the right of the 48th Division. The 11th and 22nd Reserve Infantry Divisions took over the extensions of Schwarzwaldgraben towards Thiepval, facing the remainder of the 48th and 49th Divisions. Additionally, in an attempt to aid the already tired troops of the 7th Division and to obtain a unity of authority for the defence of Pozières, the 117th Division was ordered to extend its flank eastwards to take over Pozières Trench as far as the Pozières-Contalmaison road. This extension was carried out on the night of 21 July but as a result of difficulties encountered during the relief a mixture of units remained in the line (**See map 9**). Thus by 22 July the defence of Pozières was in the hands of fresh troops on the western and south-western sides but lay with mainly tired troops to the south-eastern side.

During the night of 23 July, whilst reliefs were still going on, the British 144 Brigade (48th Division) attacked. The initial penetration was thrown back and five prisoners (one officer) and one machine gun captured. Eventually a break

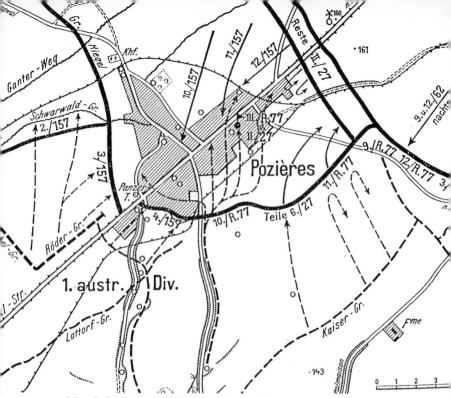

Map 9. Pozières: The German Perspective.

through was made at the junction of two units, resulting in the loss of
some 250 metres of line and a consequent fall back to the 'old'
Schwarwaldgraben. Meanwhile men of 1 Australian Brigade managed
to penetrate between 4/157 and 10/R77 at the southern end of the
village. The remnants of 6/27, in an effort to avoid being cut off,
retreated to a point north-east of Pozières. The break also permitted the
Australians to penetrate to the rear of the defenders in the Panzerturm,
Gibraltar, who continued to be heard firing until 6 a.m. when they were
finally overpowered and the tower fell silent. A further attack on
11/R77 was initially repulsed, with heavy casualties to the defenders,
but such was the determination of the attackers that the position was
eventually lost.

At 3.30 a.m. 23 July the staff of III/62 arrived at the battle
headquarters of III/R77 and II/27, just to the south of the main road, to
relieve the former. So heavy was the artillery fire that the headquarters
staff were entirely ignorant of the progress of the Australians. Not until
3.40 a.m. did a runner manage to get through to report that enemy
troops had been seen close to the headquarters position. By daybreak
it was clear that the situation in the village was critical. Part of

headquarters moved back, but some members of the staff of III/62 were captured, along with medical staff who remained in the Medical Dugout near Tramway Trench.

In an attempt to retake lost ground III/157, lying in reserve at Courcelette, was ordered to counter attack at 5.30 a.m. leaving one company, 9/157, at Courcelette to act as artillery protection. The 10th 11th and 12/157 attacked to the north of the village but were repulsed by superior machine gun fire.

To prevent permanent occupation of Pozières, the divisional commander ordered further counter-attacks to be carried out. The 157th and 27th Infantry Regiments were ordered to retake the village as soon as possible. As a precursor, the divisional artillery was instructed to hold the areas to the south and south-west of the village under continuous fire and to lay a fire block in front of the 7th Division to prevent Australian reinforcements moving up. It was this barrage which fell on Casualty Corner and Contalmaison Valley during 23 July. The combined attack was scheduled for 6.30 p.m. but during the day it became clear that the artillery had not contained the Australians and the plan was abandoned.

During the night the divisional commander expressed the opinion that the counter-attack must be carried out at once or the opportunity to stop the enemy consolidating his gains in the village and to the western defences would be lost. New reserves were constantly being brought into the rear areas so that the commander was able to send forward other units of the 157th to relieve the tired I/157 and to carry out two counter-attacks. The first was to be made on the British in the Schwarzwaldgraben by the

Pozières church taken when occupied by the Germans in 1915.

The ruined church in Pozières in September 1916. IWM Q1087

In an enemy open gun-emplacement lies a German field-gun destroyed by British shell-fire.

11th Reserve Infantry Regiment and the second on Pozières village by 7th, 9th, and remnants of the 10th, 11th and 12th companies of the 157th. Of these two attacks the first made some gains but did not retake all lost ground but the second was postponed. The conditions in the German rear areas were so bad that the projected relief of I/157 could not be effected.

In the opinion of the German staff the reason for the failure of the counter-attacks was inadequate preparation by their artillery, whose bombardments had left their opponents well able to carry out defensive actions. Accordingly at 8.25 a.m. on 24 July orders were given for a further bombardment of the whole village with the exception of the north-west corner, where the 157th still had a footing. The Australian advance was now beginning to threaten the position of the left flank of 11/Reserve Infantry Regiment which was reinforced from Thiepval. The two companies so relieved were moved into the Ganter Weg (Fourth Avenue) and Gierich Weg (Fifth Avenue) which were support lines of the Schwarzwaldgraben. The 117th Division had now deployed all its units in a series of positions to prevent the English and Australians extending their gains up to Hill 160 (the windmill). At noon on 24 July General der Infanterie von Boehn, commanding general of IX Reserve Corps, was charged with the recovery of Pozières and took over responsibility for all troops to be used in operations against it. The task of taking the village was delegated to Major-General Wellmann of the 18th Reserve Division, which took over the front previously held by the 7th Division. The main strike force, two battalions of the 86th Reserve Infantry Regiment, would attack between the Albert-Bapaume road and the Pozières-Martinpuich road, whilst the third battalion would attack in the 157th sector north of the main road. The attack was to take place at 4.30 a.m. on 25 July after a four hour concentrated barrage.

However, before Wellmann could launch his counter-attack events occurred which rendered the 86th unfit to take part. At about 5.00 a.m. a party of Australians was reported to be advancing in the region of K Trench. In reality this was only a movement up the trench but the report that reached the German headquarters suggested a much heavier action and in response the second battalion of the 86th sent two companies, the 7th and 8th, forward to reinforce the line. As they came over from the direction of the mill towards the OG Lines they were caught in machine gun and artillery fire and almost annihilated. A similar fate befell the first battalion. Fearing that an Australian advance would jeopardise Courcelette, the 1/86 Reserve Infantry Regiment was ordered to take up a position in the OG Line in front of the south-west corner of the village. As it left the village it was caught in the same hail of fire which had devastated the II/86 Reserve Infantry Regiment. As if this was not sufficient, 3/86 Reserve Infantry Regiment and 4/86 Reserve Infantry Regiment were ordered to support the second battalion and were also badly mauled as they in turn left Courcelette. Finally, the third battalion in reserve at La Sars was hurried forward in response to the same report. The 10/86 Reserve Infantry Regiment managed to get as far as the windmill before it was pinned down, but the remaining companies only reached a sunken road between Martinpuich and Courcelette before they were subject to the fierce bombardment which stopped further progress. Thus three battalions of the 86/R.I.R. were rendered hors de combat by an erroneous report.

It was not until mid afternoon that the state of the units became clear and the proposed counter-attack called off. Subsequently plans

Men of the 1st Anzac Division photographed between Pozières and La Boisselle on their return from taking Pozières on 23rd July 1916. IWM Q4040

were made for it to be carried out at 8.30 p.m. but the order was countermanded by General von Boehn who realised that he was in no position to retake Pozières without unacceptable losses of men and vast expenditure of munitions. No further attempts were made and Pozières remained in British hands until 1918.

Bibliography

1. War Diary Reserve Army. Public Record Office. WO 95 /518
2. Ibid.
3. Areas on trench maps are divided into rectangles, identified by letters and each of these is subdivided into squares identified by numbers. Thus on map 5 all the squares are in rectangle X. The squares are further subdivided into squares a, b, c and d. Thus the Chalk Pit is in square X.10.c. and Pearl Wood is in X.17.b. For greater accuracy the sides of each small square are assumed to be divided into ten, and then reading *along* and *up* to find a particular point. Thus the Chalk Pit is X.10.c 4.5 and Pearl Wood is X.17.b 9.8 On maps and in documents such positions are often identified as point 45 or point 98.
4. Lieutenant Thurnhill was killed in action 6/11/16. He is buried in Caterpillar Valley Cemetery.
5. *The Official History of Australia in the War 1914-1918.* Volume III. Bean. 1929.
6. *Nulli Secundus: History of 2nd Battalion AIF*. Taylor & Cusack. 1942.
7. Captain James is buried in Becourt Military Cemetery.
8. *The History of the First Battalion AIF 1914-1919.* Ed. Stacy, Kindon & Chedgey 1931.
9. *The Story of the Twelth: A record of the 12th Battalion AIF.* Newton. 1925.
10. *The Official History of Australia in the War 1914-1918.* Volume III. Bean. 1929.
11. Ibid.
12. *Private Papers of Douglas Haig 1914-19*. Ed. Blake 1952.
13. Major Cunningham is unusually buried in London Cemetery & Extension, High Wood, Longueval and commemorated on the Villers-Bretonneux Memorial.
14. Lieutenant Cherry was to win the Victoria Cross at Lagnicourt in March 1917.
15. *The Official History of Australia in the War 1914-1918.* Volume III. Bean. 1929.
16. Readers requiring further information on the German Army are referred to the following publications:
(a) *Handbook of the German Army in War. April 1918* Imperial War Museum Reprint 1996
(b) *The German Forces in the Field November 1918.* Imperial War Museum Reprint 1995.
(c) *Histories of Two Hundred and Fifty-One Divisions of the German Army which participated in the Great War 1914-1918.* Naval & Military Press Reprint. 1989.

Chapter Three

ACTIONS ADJACENT TO THE AUSTRALIANS

Attack by 48th Division

The 48th (South Midland) Division was a Territorial Force Division. Raised mainly in the counties of Gloucestershire, Warwickshire and Worcestershire it had its headquarters at Warwick. At the outbreak of the war it was mobilised and after a period of intense training left for France in March 1915. It remained on the Western Front until 21 March 1917 when it moved to the Italy for the remainder of the war. In July 1916 it was part of VIII Corps, Reserve Army, commanded by Major-General R. Fanshaw.

On 21 July the division was in trenches in front of Ovillers between the main road and the track running up to Pozières **(See map 10)**. Orders issued that evening required new advanced trenches to be dug during the night and for an attack to be launched by 144 and 145 Brigades in conjunction with the Australians on the night of 22/23 July. 144 Brigade was to advance west of the railway to point 47, send a flank party to capture point 90 and attempt to capture point 40 from the west and north. Point 23, between points 40 and 94, was also to be captured.[1]

145 Brigade was to advance in two columns; the right to capture the area 97, 81, 54 and 11 including the trench between 28 and 11 and as much as possible of trench 11-54. The left was to capture area 40-79 and to join hands with the right hand column north and in trench 79-11. The triangle formed by points 11-79-28 was to be left clear but to be fired upon by Stokes mortars and machine guns. The front for the attacks ran along the line 78-02-51-93-31-66.

144 Brigade attack [2]

The 6/Gloucesters were ordered to attack in the direction of point

View of the ground near Pozières. August 1916. TAYLOR LIBRARY

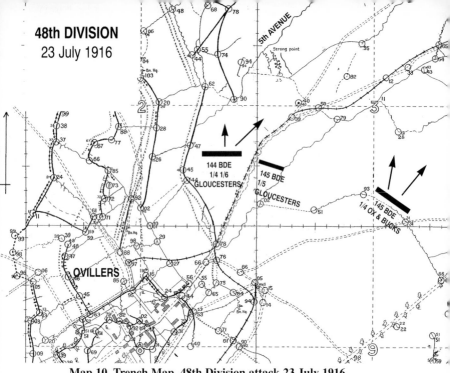

Map 10. Trench Map, 48th Division attack 23 July 1916.

94 from a position between point 47 and the railway to the east. They were to detach parties to take points 90 and 40, the latter also being attacked by 145 Brigade. C Company and half of A Company were to attack point 94 and to the right of the point 94 including point 40. The remainder of A Company were to be detached to take point 90. The attack was to be supported by three platoons of D Company on the right hand side and by one platoon of the same Company on the left. To assist with the positioning for the attack a tape was to be laid from point 47 due east, by the Royal Engineers.

In the War Diary the Commanding Officer of the 6/Gloucesters states in his report on the attack launched at 12.30 a.m. 23 July:

> *The battalion moved through Ovillers along the road and emerged at point 78. They proceeded in single file along the left of the railway and formed up on the tape. The area over which they had to move was being shelled with 5.9s but the men behaved well and the Companies moved into the assaulting formation without a hitch. At 12.15 a.m. they started moving forward and although the shelling continued there were few casualties. Shortly before zero the leading waves were roughly*

70 yards from their objective and still moving steadily. At this point machine gun fire was opened from the front and from about 39 and 40 on the right. The fire was very accurate and the leading waves were cut down. The subsequent waves carried on but very few got through the zone of fire of the machine guns. As far as we can gather from the statements of the few NCOs and men who returned a party of about 6 men entered the enemy trench just north west of point 40 and engaged the enemy with bombs. One of the party has returned. He states that he was captured and his equipment and bomb bag taken away. However, in the excitement he managed to get a bomb out of his pocket and in the confusion escaped. All officers but one who started out are casualties and information is difficult to obtain but it seems that the last waves did not get into the zone of the machine gun fire. They state that they saw the whole of the unit on the right retire and retired after them'.

The Colonel goes on explain that in his opinion,

'the failure of the attack was due to lack of artillery preparation - machine guns and men were not shelled at all. The barrage to be carried out at the same time as the attack was quite useless, no shell exploded on the front'.[3]

Among the officers killed was Lieutenant R.E.P Paramore 1/Devons (attached) commanding A Company 'who led his men as if on the barrack square'. He was eventually hit in the stomach but continued to lead until he fell dead. He is commemorated on the Thiepval Memorial.

On the left of the 6/Gloucesters the 4/Gloucesters were ordered to support by bombing northwards from point 47 and point 28. In front of point 28 the enemy were in great strength and after bombing forward for a few bays wire was encountered, although the bombing continued throughout the night. About 5.00 a.m. it was learned that the attack by the 6/Gloucesters had failed and the bombing halted.

145 Brigade attack [4]

The attack was led by the 5/Gloucesters on the left and 4/Ox & Bucks Light Infantry on the right at 12.30 a.m. The latter battalion reached point 97, where they bombed out the occupants and fought their way up the captured trench towards point 81. At the same time a direct attack was made on point 81 where the enemy broke and fled back towards Pozières carrying a machine gun but leaving the tripod and belt. At point 28 the initial attack by a platoon of A Company, led by Captain Jones, was at first held up and he called for support Resuming the attack, a very heavy hand to hand fight developed but eventually the ground was taken between 1.30 and 2.00 a.m.

On the left the attackers were met by a barrage of bombs when still some way from their objective - the trench running west from point 28 to 81 - and suffered many casualties. A party led by Sergeant Clark managed to get into the trench but were shortly forced to retire following a fierce enemy counter-attack. The brigade war diary states that there were difficulties in getting information from the Ox & Bucks but a request for support was received and at 2.52 a.m. One company of the Royal Berkshires was placed at their disposal. At 3.55 a.m. further messages indicated that the situation had deteriorated and Captain Aldworth was despatched with two companies from trenches in the vicinity of point 66. The supporting troops moved forward 'as if on parade' across a barrage of shells and intense machine gun fire. The objective was reached and the trench captured and consolidated. For the remainder of the day the captured trenches were held by the Royal Berkshires and the Ox & Bucks and from mid-day until dusk were subjected to a fierce bombardment mainly by 15cm shells and both units suffered heavy casualties

Meanwhile the 5/Goucesters attacked on a front between points 02 to 79 on the right and the railway on the left; their objectives were to capture points 79 and 40 and then to join hands with the 4/Ox & Bucks in trench 79 to 11. Unfortunately the direction of the attack was quickly discovered by the enemy who were holding the section of trench concerned very strongly. A heavy artillery barrage was brought down upon the attackers, supported by machine gun fire. Although reinforcements were moved up the attack, even after further artillery bombardment of the German lines, failed. At 3.30 a.m. the battalion was withdrawn to reserve, being relieved by the 1/Bucks Battalion who had moved up from reserve positions outside Ovillers. Among the casualties was Second Lieutenant W.B. Lycett 8/Northants (attached) who died of his wounds on 24 July. He is buried at Gézaincourt Communal Cemetery Extension. (Doullens)

At 5.20 a.m. the 1/Bucks Battalion was ordered to continue the attack at 6.30 a.m. They made their way up to communication trenches, D Company on the right and B Company on the left, under orders to extend inwards and then jointly rush the German line. D Company moved to their jumping off trench, extended and attacked before the British barrage lifted. Their war diary states [5] 'it was entirely due to this fact that they were able to carry out successfully what two other enterprises had failed to accomplish.' This belief was later confirmed by a captured German officer who stated that they were taken completely by surprise and were waiting for the British barrage to lift.

Meanwhile B Company under Captain O.V. Viney were seriously impeded by our own barrage, their casualties being so great, including Captain Viney, that they were forced to withdraw and took no part in the attack. A Company in support of D entered the German trench and linked up with D Company. Consolidation was immediately commenced and a bombing section moved to the right to make contact with the 4/Royal Berkshires. During the afternoon a bombing section reached point 40 and advanced some 90 yards up the German trench but were forced back by rifle grenades and an artillery barrage.

Attack by 12th Division

The 12th (Eastern Division) was a New Army division raised from men of the Eastern and Home Counties. It arrived in France in June 1915.

On the night of 24/25 July 1916 the division was transferred to II Corps, which by this time was part of the Reserve Army. In conjunction with the Australian Corps on its right, the division was ordered to push forward towards Thiepval from the ground recently won by the 48th Division. Accordingly, on the morning of 28 July, the division commenced to relieve the 48th. 37 Brigade took over the left flank and 36 the right **(See map 11)**. These units were ordered to attack 4th Avenue from point 95 to K Trench at 11.00 p.m. on 3 August. The

Map 11. Trench Map, 12th Division attack 3 August 1916.

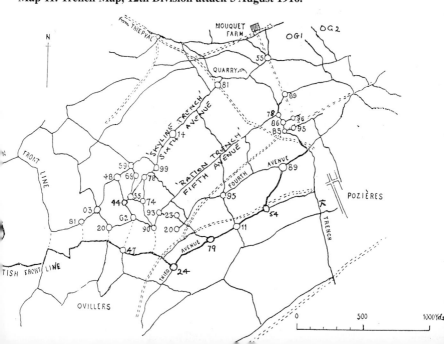

Flammenwerfer **discharge on the Western Front.** IWM Q29905

British front line now ran from point 47 to 3rd Avenue point 24 and thence to points 79-11-54-89. In preparation, 36 Brigade extended their line by bombing down 4th Avenue to the road just past point 95.[6] The line to be attacked, along with the adjacent strong points and communication trenches, was bombarded for several hours and following a five minute intense barrage, the 8/Royal Fusiliers and the 6/East Kents (Buffs) attacked. All objectives were taken including the trench from point 95 to point 20 and a strong point at point 23. Some of the Fusiliers also found their way into the trench between points 23 and 93, where they were subsequently joined by men of the Buffs.

So successful was the operation that the 8/Royal Fusiliers were ordered to move on to 5th Avenue and to bomb up to join the 7/Royal Sussex, already in K Trench, at point 78. This attack failed to capture point 78 but some ground was gained in 5th Avenue at point 93.

On the following night 4/5 August, the attack on 5th Avenue was renewed. 36 Brigade attacked with three battalions in the line. On the right, the 7/Royal Sussex attacked point 78 and 200 yards of 5th Avenue, in the centre the 9/Royal Fusiliers attacked just the trench while on the left the 8/Royal Fusiliers bombed up the trench from ground captured on the previous night, point 93. 37 Brigade on the left also attacked but with only two battalions. The 6/Royal Warwicks were to capture point 90 and join up with the British front at point 47 whilst the 6/Queens bombed forward from point 90 to point 47. All assaults were launched at 9.15 p.m. and were successful with the exception of that on point 78. During the following day a substantial number of Germans surrendered, having been trapped in the maze of trenches between 4th and 5th Avenues. The success of the two actions led to a message of congratulation from General Gough.

The next night the enemy launched a counter-attack described in the History of the Royal Fusiliers:

'Shortly before midnight a heavy bombardment of the lines began and the shelling continued until 4 a.m. (6th). The 9th

The Australian attacks on the nights of July 29 and August 4 were delivered, in the main, from west to east (i.e., from left to right across the picture) against the O.G. Lines. When these lines had been captured the subsequent advances were directed northwards, towards Mouquet Farm. The photograph was taken some time after their occupation by the Australians and Canadians, and shortly after the line had been finally advanced beyond this point. It shows the entrance of one of the many dugouts in these trenches.

Battalion lying west of the 8th were subjected to a determined counter-attacking this time. Many of the men were quite new to warfare. For some it was their first experience of actual fighting, and their bearing was admirable. The assault was made by flammenwerfer, supported by bombers using smoke as a screen. The flames burst through the clouds of smoke from various directions, all the conditions for panic were present. The fumes alone were sufficient to overpower men. But no panic took place. The situation was handled very coolly. The attack was made on the north-east end of Ration Trench, and about 20 men were extended in the open on either side of the trench with two Lewis guns. The attack was thus beaten off with a loss of only 40 yards of trench. Many fine incidents marked this defence. Private Leigh Rouse (awarded MM), who had never visited trenches before, was in a sap when the flammenwerfer attack began. He managed to get back along the trench and though nearly choked with fumes and his clothes burnt, refused to go to the dressing station. He continued to throw bombs until his arm gave out, and then, joining the covering party , used his rifle with great effect '.[7]

A further attempt to take point 78, by three companies of the 7/Suffolks, 35 Brigade which had replaced 36, on 8 August was unsuccessful and so on the 9th all troops were cleared from the trench running between points 85 and 95 and a heavy bombardment was laid down on point 78 and adjacent trenches, after which troops of the Australian 4th Division finally captured this troublesome point. They were immediately joined by men of the 7/Suffolks to complete the line.

Operations to capture 6th Avenue and the ground opposite 37 Brigade were set for the night of 12/13 August. As the width of No Man's Land between 5th and 6th Avenues was considered to be excessive, forward trenches were dug to be accessed via saps from 5th Avenue. In the event this probably saved many lives as the enemy counter-barrage fell directly on 5th Avenue. The attack is described in the History of the 12th Division:

'Zero hour was 10.30 p.m., and after three minutes intense bombardment the 7/Norfolk Regiment, with "A" and "B" Companies in front and "D" and "C" Companies in support, dashed forward, and captured their portion, the right of 6th Avenue, at 10.40 p.m. So rapid was their advance that touch on the flanks was temporarily lost. "C" Company, however, worked down the trench to the left and gained touch with the 9/Essex at about 11.40 p.m., and at midnight touch was also gained with the

Australian 4th Division, which had gained its objective, at point 81. Patrols pushed forward, but were held up by our artillery barrage. Few casualties were incurred and seventeen prisoners were taken. The 9/Essex Regiment attacking on the left of the Norfolk Regiment, with "C" and "D" Companies and "A" in support, captured their objective, 6th Avenue, as far as point 78, with little opposition. Patrols were sent to the left to obtain touch with the 7/East Surreys. Trench 78-74 was found to be almost obliterated, and after advancing about 75 yards along 78-55 strong opposition was met and a barricade made. A bombing party from 99 reached 59 and formed a block there'.[8]

On the left, the attack by 37 Brigade was less successful. On the right of this sector the objective of the 7/East Surreys was the area bounded by the points 74, 55, 44 and 62. They were also required to make contact with the Essex at point 78. (At the south-west end of 6th Avenue. Do not confuse with the point 78 where K Trench joins 5th Avenue). D Company failed to find point 74 due to the state of the ground and under heavy machine gun and artillery fire became totally lost. A few troops reached point 44 and some others made contact at point 78. B company attacked point 68 but was driven back as was the reserve, A company. At the same time the 6/Royal West Kents assaulted the strong points 20 and 81. So effective was the German defence that the attack was brought to a standstill.

Again according to the History of the 12th Division:

'The battle of the night had resulted in the capture of the German position on a front of 1000 yards to an average depth of 400 yards'.

During the following day the division was progressively relieved by the 48th Division.

British Attacks 23 July 1916

The Australians, the right of the Reserve Army, were established in Black Watch Alley by the morning of 21 July and had taken over their portion of OG 1 that lay beyond this trench. The Australians and the troops of the 1st Division were almost back-to-back at their point of junction. Here there existed a salient both difficult to defend and unsuitable as a position from which to launch an attack.

As the Australians attacked at Pozières the Fourth Army carried out a series of attacks stretching from the junction with the Australians past High Wood to Longueval and Guillemont (**See map 12**). The three Corps concerned were the III, XV and XIII.

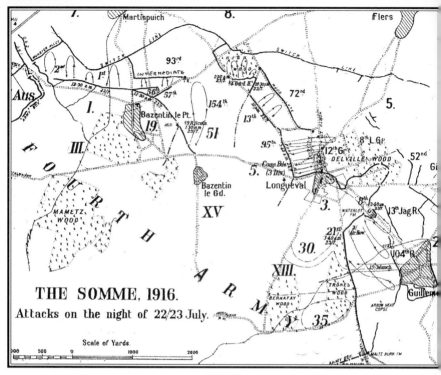

Map 12. Fourth Army attacks, 22/23 July 1916. (Based on Official History Map).

III Corps

The Corps held the ground adjacent to the Australians and used the 1st and 19th Divisions to attack at 12.30 a.m. 23 July. For both divisions the objective was the extension of OG 2, which after its junction with Munster Alley was referred to as the Switch Line. It ran in front of Martinpuich, through the north-eastern tip of High Wood and then between Flers and Ginchy south-eastwards towards Morval.

The 1st Division attacked from positions out in No Man's Land with 2 and 1 Brigades. 2 Brigade attacked where the Switch Line formed a re-entrant at its junction with Munster Alley. Neither of its battalions, the 2/King's Royal Rifle Corps nor the 2/Royal Sussex, managed to reach the Switch Line. The same was true for the two battalions of 1 Brigade, 1/Cameron Highlanders and 10/Gloucesters. Both brigades suffered heavily from enfilade machine gun fire and were forced to withdraw. On their right the two brigades of the 19th Division, 56 and 57 were caught in artillery fire when getting up to the front line. The Divisional History records the misfortune of the support battalion of 56 Brigade.

> *'The guides supplied by the 98th Brigade did not altogether excel themselves especially in the case of the 7th Royal Lancaster Regiment... the four guides took the battalion right up to the front line. As, of course, there was no battalion for them to relieve, the 7th Royal Lancasters were eventually marched back to their exact position'.* [9]

All this was under heavy fire which took an inevitable toll, in this case, two officers and 40 other ranks.

The portion of the Switch Line designated as the objective of the 19th Division was the section between the road running from Martinpuich to Bazentin le Petit to the north-west edge of High Wood. Shortly before the attack the existence of an hitherto unknown trench, running south and east out of the Switch Trench, was confirmed. This trench, Intermediate Trench, had now to be captured before the Switch Line could be reached. Another last minute change forced on the division was the replacement of the 10/Worcesters, in 57 Brigade line, with the 10/Royal Warwicks. The Worcesters were thought to be unfit to lead the attack after being involved in several preliminary skirmishes.

Again quoting the Divisional History:

> *'At 12.30 a.m. (23rd July) the 56th and 57th Brigades attacked the enemy, but very little progress was made owing to the heavy machine gun fire from the front and from the right flank. By 6.55 a.m. the attacking troops were back in their original trenches'.* [10]

XVCorps

Further to the right still the 51st and 5th Divisions attacked either side of High Wood, the 5th in an attempt to take Wood Lane, the German trench running from the south-eastern side of the wood down towards Delville Wood and the Switch line beyond, the 51st to capture the wood itself and 600 yards of the Switch Line adjoining it on the north-west. Of the attack, the History of the 5th Division says:

> *'At 10 p.m., after a bombardment, the 13th Brigade advanced to the attack against Wood Lane, the West Kents attacking on the right, and the 14th Warwicks on the left. They met a heavy counter-barrage and streams of lead from numerous machine guns and, after suffering severe casualties, were forced to retire to their jumping off line. A further attack was ordered for 1.30 a.m., the objectives being again Wood Lane, and afterwards Switch Trench. The attack was postponed till 3.30 a.m., and met with the same result as before'.* [11]

The 51st Division at 1.30 a.m., using 154 Brigade, advanced. Following the attacks of 13 Brigade and those of the 19th Division the enemy was awaiting any further advances. The 4/Gordon Highlanders and 9/Royal Scots suffered heavily. The Gordons entered the remains of the wood but were driven out by machine guns in the Switch Line, while the Royal Scots were enfiladed from Intermediate Trench. Both retired and by 3.30 am. were back in their starting trenches although many men never lived to see these lines again. The joint casualty figures amounted to some 450 officers and other ranks.

On the extreme right of the Fourth Army the XIII Corps attacked at 3.40. a.m. The objectives for the 3rd Division were Longueval, Delville Wood and Guillemont Station whilst that for the 30th Division was Guillemont village. Neither attack involved the Switch Line and so will not be considered, but in common with the other attacks by the Fourth Army were unsuccessful.

Bibliography
1. War Diary 48th Division. Public Record Office. WO 95/2760
2. War Diary 144 Infantry Brigade. Public Record. Office. WO 95/2757
3. War Diary 1/6th Gloucesters. Public Record Office. WO 95/2758
4. War Diary 145 Infantry Brigade. Public Record Office. WO 95/2760
5. War Diary 1/1st Bucks Battalion Ox. & Bucks L.I. Public Record Office. WO 95/2763
6. War Diary 36 Brigade. Public Record Office. WO 95/1854.
7. *The History of the Royal Fusiliers in the Great War.* O'Neill. Heinemann. 1922.
8. *History of the 12th Division in the Great War.* Scott & Brumwell. Nisbet 1923.
9. *The History of the 19th Division 1914-1918.* Wyrall. Edward Arnold 1922
10. Ibid
11. *The Fifth Division in the Great War.* Hussey & Inman Nisbet 1921.

Chapter Four

THE AUSTRALIANS ON THE SOMME II

Mouquet Farm

General Gough now turned his attention to driving northwards along the ridge towards Thiepval. He planned to take Mouquet Farm and then move on to the 'Zollern Work' half a mile further north. The Australian front line was now a salient and consequently the German artillery was able to bombard what was a short line from three sides. The length of the front also restricted the number of men that could be employed in an attack to brigade size and frequently only to part thereof.

The next phase of the advance was set for 9.20 p.m. on 8 August. On the left the British 12th Division was to take point 78, the junction of K Trench and 5th Avenue. Several earlier attempts had failed due to heavy machine gun fire from the road running up to Mouquet Farm. At the same time the Australians would attack Park Lane. The continual bombardments from both sides had rendered the ground between Pozières and the farm unrecognisable, a fact that would become all too clear to the Australians after the attack was completed. The 15th Battalion was given the task and, as the preliminary barrage lifted and the enemy machine guns concentrated on the attack upon point 78, swept forward over the 200 yards which separated the lines and,

Mouquet Farm lay about a mile north of Pozières. It was the country residence of the owner of a local factory. The Germans in fortifying it excavated dugouts under the main farm buildings and also under the back buildings, which are those shown in this photograph. A third system of dugouts was made some distance in rear of the back buildings. TAYLOR LIBRARY

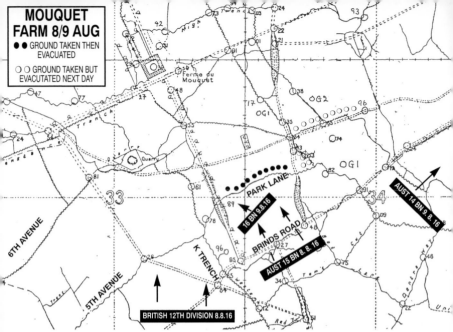

Map 13. Trench Map, Mouquet Farm, 8/9 August 1916.

finding little or no opposition, captured their objective. Unfortunately, the attack on point 78 failed and it soon became clear the Germans also still held point 96, both of which points were potentially lethal to the troops now occupying Park Lane, particularly those on the left flank. At daybreak the units on the left were withdrawn leaving the right, not in the extension of Park Lane as they thought, but well ahead as shown in **(See map 13)**. This error became very clear when, at the onset of the barrage prior to the next phase, they came under fire from their own artillery and had to retire.

Following the failure of the 12th Division to take point 78, for the renewed attack, scheduled for the following night, the task was given to the 16th Battalion. After an intense but short bombardment they successfully attacked at 12.05 a.m. from trenches in front of Brind's Road while the 15th reoccupied all the trenches in and beyond Park Lane taken the previous night. As part of a subsidiary plan to expand the right wing the 14th Battalion took points 24 and 61.

In the afternoon of the following day the 15th Battalion was relieved by the 13th Battalion and together with the 16th was ordered to continue the movement towards Mouquet Farm. There now followed a period when orders from Division where inconsistent with the situation on the ground, due in part to the state of the ground and in part to difficulties of communication with forward units even using aerial observation. Headquarters was never sure of the exact position of the front. On the night of 10/11 August the 13th Battalion was ordered to attack and capture the trench running form point 34 to point 96 which was already held. They duly carried out an operation and succeeded in capturing OG 1 up to its junction with the road east of Mouquet Farm and part of the trench running across to point 55. At the same time the 16th Battalion in K Trench captured point 61.

On the following night orders required bombing parties to capture points 38, 17, 55 and 61 two of which, 38 and 61, were already held, and to dig a jumping off trench in front of the quarry in preparation for the projected capture of the line from the quarry to point 81. At daylight on the 11th the enemy commenced a bombardment on the 16th Battalion and on 5th Avenue which continued until 2.30 p.m. when a party of Germans emerged from Mouquet Farm and advanced towards the quarry, where they sheltered in shell holes until 2.45 p.m. when they rose and continued to move southwards across the valley where they were caught in enfilade fire from Lewis guns of both the 13th and 16th Battalions. Such was the size of the German party the commander of the 16th Battalion, Lieutenant-Colonel D. Brockman, called up a heavy artillery barrage which fell upon them at the same time as the machine gun fire. The German barrage grew in intensity as the day wore on, falling not only on the ground in front of Mouquet Farm but back as far as the Chalk Pit and Sausage Valley. It was during this day that Private M. O'Meara won the fifth VC for the Australians. Needless to say the proposed jumping off trench was not dug!

The 16th Battalion suffered heavily during the bombardment so

The 6th Brigade on August 10th passing the 2nd Brigade near Warloy-Baillon. Like all the brigades which successively held Pozières, the 6th had been subjected to the heavy bombardments continually laid upon that area by the Germans. The 2nd Brigade was shortly to move thither for its second 'tour'.

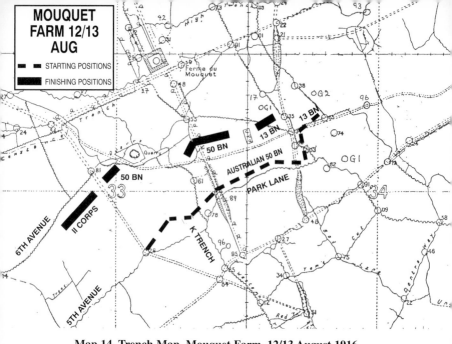

Map 14. Trench Map, Mouquet Farm, 12/13 August 1916.

before the next stage of the advance on Mouquet Farm it was taken out of the line and replaced by the 50th Battalion of 13 Brigade. This relief, carried out during 12 August while the German bombardment

Australians loading a 9.45 inch trench mortar, 'A Flying Pig', in the chalk pit south of Pozières in August 1916. IWM Q4092

continued, led to many casualties in the relieving column. The next step was to be a joint one with II Corps to be delivered at 10.30 p.m. As far as the Australians were concerned the 50th Battalion, in the absence of jumping off trenches, would attack from Park Lane and 5th Avenue whilst the 13th would be in trenches further forward and to their right **(See map 14)**. The artillery support was to be provided by the Lahore Brigades and Bean records:

> 'a continuous flash of shrapnel bursting almost over the men's foreheads'

he goes on to say that:

> 'after the torture they (the 50th Battalion) had experienced when coming up, the men were greatly cheered by the sight'.[1]

The task allotted to the 50th required that it cross a valley, a distance of about 300 yards, to reach its objective, the edge of the quarry.

II Corps captured 6th Avenue. The left company of the 50th reached point 81 but their right flank failed to reach the quarry, stopping some way short of point 55, although roughly level with the 13th Battalion. Gaps existed between the two parts of the 50th and between the left flank and the 13th Battalion. Unfortunately, the difficulty of identifying exact positions led to the 50th sending back incorrect reports of their position - they believed that they were at the objective.

During 13 August the British 12th Division on the left was replaced by the 48th. The Australian 4 Brigade, with the exception of the 13th Battalion, was relieved by the Australian 13 Brigade whose 50th

Map 15. Trench Map, Mouquet Farm, 14 August 1916.

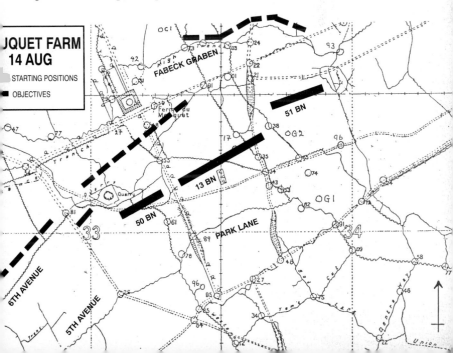

Battalion was already in the line. The 51st Battalion entered the line on the right of the 13th Battalion **(See map 15)** whilst the 50th Battalion and 13th Battalion moved to the left to reduce the gap between the 50th Battalion and its company at point 81. The 49th Battalion relieved the 14th Battalion on the right flank.

As planning proceeded for the capture of Mouquet Farm and at the same time to extend the view over Courcelette valley, calculations were upset by the recapture of 6th Avenue up to point 81 by the Germans just before midnight. Faced with this new situation plans were amended, instead of attempting to capture the farm the Australians would attack a line running from point 81, behind the quarry and up into the major trench Fabeck Graben, to the north-east. At the same time the British 48th Division would attempt to regain the ground lost in 6th Avenue. The artillery duels were continuous and the 50th Battalion in particular lost heavily in the period before the attack.

On the left the 50th got beyond the quarry but were then pinned down by machine gun fire from Constance Trench and eventually forced to retire. On the right the 51st moved upwards towards the Fabeck Graben but they too were stopped by machine gun fire from a section of the trench on higher ground. In the centre the 13th Battalion advanced along the line of OG 1 to the Fabeck Graben and then bombed along it up to its junction with OG 2, where it set up a barricade. A series of bombing attacks by the Germans were repulsed until eventually, there being no contact with units on either flank, the officer in charge, Captain H. Murray, ordered a withdrawal. In the meantime the 51st had also retired and so no gains were made except on the 48th Division front, where a large part of 6th Avenue was recaptured but not the final portion near point 81.

In actions since its entry into the line on 5 August the Australian 4th Division had suffered 4649 casualties: 132 officers and 4517 other ranks.

So the Australian rapid thrust towards Thiepval had been halted. The 4th Division was relieved on 15 August by the Australian 1st Division who returned to the fray. Before any attempt was made to renew operations Lieutenant-General Walker, commanding the division, put his staff to work on improving communications to avoid further problems of inaccurate information regarding battalion positions. Indeed so concerned were his subordinates with this problem and its effects upon troops when it lead to incorrect co-ordinates being sent to artillery units, that General Smyth (1 Brigade) himself visited the area of the quarry valley to ascertain the situation.

Even he underestimated the extent to which the line had moved forward and it was not until new aerial observations were carried out that the true locations were identified. 2 Brigade (5th and 6th Battalions) took over the ground near the windmill and 1 Brigade (3rd and 4th Battalions) took control of operations to the north. These latter battalions were given little time to settle in as the Germans had planned an attack for that day. It was delivered, following the usual increased barrage, in the early evening in the vicinity of OG 1. But was repulsed by bombs, rifle and machine gun fire.

White's orders required that he embark upon two separate actions, one eastwards in the vicinity of the Pozières windmill, which when launched by 2 Brigade at 9.00 p.m. on 18 August resulted in no gains. By the time it was relieved on 21 August the brigade had lost 24% of its manpower. The second, northwards, carried out at the same time by 1 Brigade, was little more successful. Its objectives **(See map 16)** were:

1. On the left, point 55, to be taken by the 4th Battalion.

2. On the right, a new trench in course of construction adjacent to point 22, to be taken by the 3rd Battalion.

Even though the correct position of the front line had now been established, the artillery bombardment fell upon the 3rd Battalion. The advance was lead by bombing units who either failed to achieve their objectives or had to retreat for lack of support. Only the 4th Battalion on the left was successful, where point 55 was gained.

Map 16. Trench Map, Mouquet Farm, 18 August 1916.

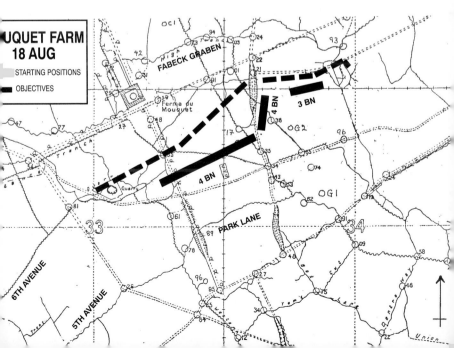

1 Brigade was relieved by the 3rd on 19 August, the fresh troops being needed before the Division embarked on plans to capture part of the Fabeck Graben. Walker decided on an operation to capture a line from point 55 to point 91, the junction of OG 1 with the road in front of the farm and then to point 73 and along the Fabeck Graben to point 95 **(See map 17)**. On this occasion he was unable to construct jumping off trenches as the troops were fully occupied digging out the main trenches which were constantly collapsing under the weight of the enemy artillery. Due to the lie of the land the Australian lines were in clear view of the enemy and any preparations were quickly registered and the ground pounded. In an attempt to mislead them the preliminary bombardment was broken up into parts. Two were delivered on the evening of 20 August, a third early on the morning of the 21st and a final one between 1.30 and 2.30 p.m. on the 21st. To cover the attack, scheduled for 5.00 p.m., a creeping barrage was to be used - two minutes in front of the Fabeck Graben, three minutes on it and then on to the ground beyond. That an attack was about to take place could not be hidden from the enemy and in the afternoon of the 21st they launched a very heavy bombardment which caused many casualties and certainly reduced the efficiency of the battalions waiting in the line and prevented the 11th from reaching its starting position until after the attack had started.

The positions allocated to the Division are shown on **(See map 17)**. On the 10th Battalion front the recurring problem of the state of the ground and the destruction of the trenches by the artillery led to some

Map 17. Trench Map, Mouquet Farm, 21 August 1916.

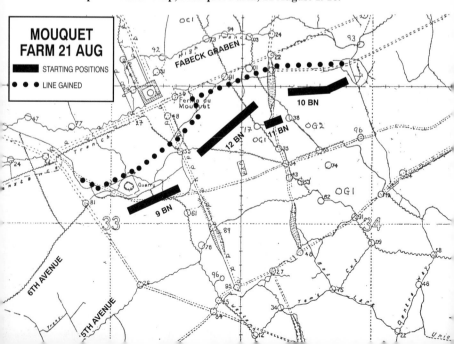

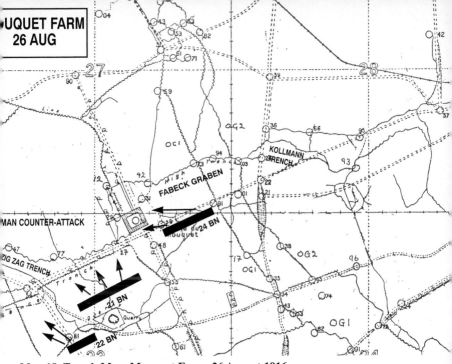

Map 18. Trench Map, Mouquet Farm, 26 August 1916.

men passing the Fabeck Graben and getting caught in their own barrage. Others entered the trench but were unable to hold it and fell back, to dig in only just in front of their original line. On their left the 12th Battalion, having been held up by the German barrage, did not attack until past midnight but reached points close to the road before being stopped by machine gun fire. The 12th Battalion initially exceeded expectations, managing to reach a point in front of Mouquet Farm and even entering the ruins, before being forced to retire during the night. The morning dawned with a heavy mist covering the landscape and hiding the division from the searching guns of the enemy. Saps were busily dug and a new front line established in the relative safety of the cloak of invisibility.

On 22 August the 1st Division was withdrawn from the line and replaced by the 2nd. In its second spell in the Pozières sector the division suffered the loss of 92 officers and 2558 other ranks.

The 2nd Division had already suffered much but 6 Brigade was considered by Brigadier-General John Gellibrand to be the least affected and was chosen to continue the push towards Mouquet Farm, with 5 Brigade holding the line facing east. Relief of 3 Brigade by the 6th took place in the late afternoon of 22 August, its three battalions from left to right being 24th, 21st and 23rd. The plan put forward by

Air photograph of Mouquet Farm. The Fabeck Graben and Zig Zag Trench are clearly visible on the top right and lower left respectively.
IWM Q1087

General White required the division on the right to bomb up to the Fabeck Graben but to concentrate on taking the ground to the west of the farm. This meant using the 24th Battalion, which was badly under strength and contained a number of replacements lacking in experience. Gellibrand decided to swap the positions of the 24th and 21st Battalions, a manoeuvre which was not easy to carry out but which was nevertheless successfully completed. The 21st Battalion was to attack at dawn under cover of a creeping barrage. The objective was a line linking points 54, 77, 27 and 12 **(See map 18)**. At the same time the 24th Battalion would attack with bombers with the object of capturing dug-outs adjacent to the farm and point 31. The left flank of the operation would be protected by a company of the 22nd Battalion who, following upon the heels of the 21st, would fan out to cover the road between points 54 and 81.

At 4.15 a.m. on 26 August the men of the 21st Battalion left the relative security of their front line trench to lie out in No Man's Land. At 4.45 a.m. they rose and followed the barrage, but in the poor light passed over Constance Trench and on to ZigZag Trench where their problems really started. As so often before the trench was undetectable and although a few troops were stopped at point 77 the majority passed over ZigZag Trench and, bearing to the right, became enmeshed in the tangle of the Mouquet Farm position. To the right of the 21st the 24th got bombers into the ground on the east side of the farm but they were driven back by machine gun fire and retaliatory bombing from Germans climbing up out of their dug-outs. Point 54 at the junction of the track leading to the farm and the road from Pozières to Thiepval was also missed by the majority of the troops designated to take it. They swung too far to the right. It was stormed by a small party under Lieutenant Oscar Jones, who attacked with bombs until lack of supplies lead them to take cover in shell holes near the strong point. The point itself was located in a cutting in the road and the Germans used the wall of the cutting as a base to set up two machine guns which poured fire into the area around the farm.

At 7.30 a.m. the Germans counter-attacked down from the direction of Thiepval but, being observed from the rear Australian lines, were beaten back by mortar fire. By the end of the day, when the 21st Battalion was relieved, it had lost 13 officers and 440 other ranks. The Brigade lost 36% of its strength. The attack had been an attempt to

Air photograph of Mouquet Farm after further artillery action.

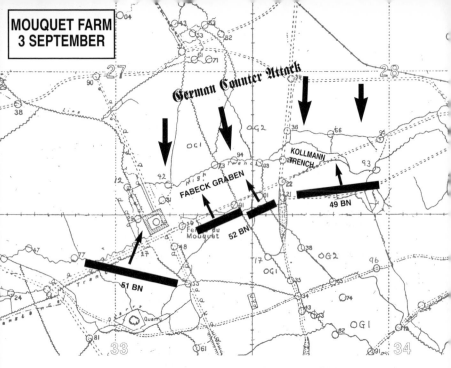

Map 19. Trench Map, Mouquet Farm, 26 August 1916.

straighten the Australian front but had not succeeded, the only gain being point 77 which was consolidated by the relieving battalion.

For administrative reasons the 2nd Division now briefly took over 4 Brigade which relieved 6 Brigade. At noon on 28 August the 4th Division formally replaced the 2nd Division with the 13th and 16th Battalions in the line relieving the 14th and 15th Battalions which had been there since the failure of the last attack. No further attempt was made to straighten the line, General White deciding to use the 4th Division to capture the farm and the line running from point 54 through points 77, 12, 42, 73, 94, 36 to point 95 in an attack using a whole brigade. He argued that previous attacks had failed to capture the farm, after getting into the area around it, due to the superior numbers of German defenders. Therefore the use of a whole brigade would give depth to the attack. Cox, the 4th Division commander, disagreed stating that two battalions would suffice. White reluctantly agreed - a mistake!

The weather now took a hand. It rained solidly, turning shell holes into hideous oily pools and earth into glutinous mud which made movement difficult, especially at a fixed rate behind a creeping barrage. In the ensuing attack at 11 p.m. on 29 August, rifles, Lewis guns and even bombs were rendered useless, becoming clogged with mud. The 13th Battalion **(See map 18)** quickly took a partly constructed trench, Kollmann Trench and some got into the Fabeck Graben between points 73 and 94. The 16th Battalion failed to take point 54 and many, like the 21st before them, got lost and separated. There followed a series of isolated fights at points 42, 31 and 12, some of which changed hands several times before the Australians were forced back with the remnants of the 13th finally dislodged from point 73. No ground was won and when the roll was called, after the two battalions were relieved on the 30th, they had jointly lost 19 officers and 440 other ranks.

The final attempt by the Australians to capture Mouquet Farm was launched at 5.10 a.m. on 3 September. It was part of a joint offensive by the Reserve Army against Thiepval and the Fourth Army further to the east. The 4th Division was now the only Australian division on the Somme, the 1st and the 2nd having been moved back to Ypres. The strength of the division was increased by the arrival of 1 Canadian Brigade, which came under the command of the Australians on 30 August and relieved 7 Brigade to the east of Pozières. For the attack 13 Brigade was to be used with the 51st, 52nd and 49th Battalions in the line, attacking the farm, the Fabeck Graben and the farm from the left, and the Fabeck Graben respectively. The 50th Battalion was in reserve **(See map 19)**. To ensure that the three attacking battalions were fresh, the digging of new assembly and communication trenches was delegated to other units. The orders given to the 51st stated that it must attack 'in strength and depth'.

The creeping barrage was a complicated one, needing to help both the capture of the farm and the Fabeck Graben further back. On the extreme right the 49th Battalion made good progress in successive waves, and although suffering heavy casualties, most of the officers being killed or wounded, occupied the area bounded by points 36-95-93-03. On the right the first waves of the 51st Battalion progressed to a line just in front of the Fabeck Graben whilst succeeding ones dealt with the honeycomb of dug-outs in and around the ruins of the farm buildings. In this they were aided by the left wing of the 52nd Battalion. The main body of the 52nd Battalion was held up by a machine gun supported by bombers in nearby shell holes. Eventually, the gun was eliminated and the 52nd linked up with the 49th Battalion and sheltered in the remains of Kollmann Trench. Other units managed to get into the Fabeck Graben between points 42 and 73 and between the OG Lines.

At 8.00 a.m. on 3 September large numbers of Germans were seen to be moving down towards point 42 between the 51st and 52nd Battalions. At the same time the Germans launched a heavy artillery barrage on to the farm. The 52nd fell back leaving the 51st isolated. Bean quotes a message sent back by Lieutenant A. Clifford, the last heard of the men in that forward position:

'Being hard pressed. Enemy bombing up our trench from both ends. Strong Point to our left rear (12) has not been cleared, as they are sniping from our rear. Trench half-full of wounded and dead...only about 30 men with me. No sign of communication trench to us from the farm as yet. Lost trace of 52nd'.[2]

Bean notes that some eight years later the War Graves Commission found a trench in front of the farm containing a number of Australian bodies, almost certainly the remains of Clifford and his men.

The Germans swept on, retaking the farm and forcing the Australians to retire to their starting lines, with the exception of the 49th Battalion and its supporting members of the 52nd on the extreme right. A 3.30 p.m. a company of 13 Canadian Brigade was sent up the sunken road between points 34 and 22 to assist the hard pressed and weary 52nd Battalion. General Gough, now aware that of all the elements of the attack only the gains made by the 49th Battalion were significant, ordered that a line be consolidated linking the high ground of the 49th with the line in front of the farm. The Australians and Canadians fought off German attempts to break through and succeeded in holding part of the Fabeck Graben from point 66 through 95 to 93 until relieved the next day. The 52nd Battalion was relieved by the Canadian 16th Battalion who managed, by use of bombs, to forge the link required.

On 3 September, whilst the battle was still in progress, General Birdwood and the Anzac Corps had handed over to General Byng, commander of the Canadian Corps, and on the 4th the commander of the 1st Canadian Division, Major-General A. Currie, relieved General Cox of the Australian 4th Division.

In this final tour the 4th Division lost 41 officers and 1305 other ranks.

As stated in the Official History:

'Australia has every reason to be proud of the devotion and gallantry of her troops in the fiery ordeal of the Somme battle...the men had proved themselves skilful and self-reliant - if at times over reckless - fighters, and their leaders were quick to

benefit by their experience of offensive warfare on the Western Front. [3]

General Gough also paid tribute to the Australians:

'The Australian officers and men had shown a fine spirit, not only in attack, but in the steady courage which is required to stand up to constant shelling day and night and to repel frequent counter-attacks. Their commander, General Birdwood, was always easy to work with. Their Chief Staff Officer, Brudenell White, was most capable, highly trained, possessing great tact and sound judgement which made him one of the best Staff Officers we had in the Army'. [4]

The Capture of Mouquet Farm

During the day and night of 4 September the Germans launched four weak counter-attacks. Sir Douglas Haig had suggested that the Canadians be given time to settle in before being involved in a major action but those Canadians in front of Mouquet Farm during the days 5-8 September found them extremely arduous. 3 Brigade suffered under heavy artillery fire and frequent counter-attacks. When relieved on 8 September the Germans chose the exact same time to counter-attack yet again and managed to win back a section of the Fabeck

Ruins of Mouquet Farm in October 1916.

Graben in the vicinity of point 66. By this time the Canadian 1st Division held the whole of the Corps front whilst the 2nd and 3rd Divisions were preparing to enter the scene. The front, made up of very battered trenches, ran for about 3000 yards from the junction with the Fourth Army at Munster Alley to a point 700 yards west of Mouquet Farm. At 4.45 p.m. on 9 September the 2nd Battalion launched an attack on the German front line either side of the railway track between the main road and Munster Alley. As described in the Official History:

> '*After hand to hand fighting the objective was secured on a frontage of 500 yards and more than sixty prisoners of the 211th Reserve Regiment were sent back. The new line was mercilessly shelled by the enemy, who delivered several counter-attacks all of which were repulsed'.* [5]

It was during this action that Corporal L Clarke won the Victoria Cross.

> '*He attacked, almost single-handed a party of twenty Germans and routed them, capturing one after he had received a bayonet thrust in the leg'.*

On 15 September the Battle of Flers-Courcelette opened on a front which extended for some 10 miles from Thiepval to Combles. The task of the Reserve Army was twofold, to attack Courcelette astride the Albert-Bapaume road and to protect the left flank. The attack on Courcelette was to be delivered by the 2nd Division while the 3rd Division provided the protection. 8 Brigade held the whole 3rd Division front from a point on the Courcelette track **(See map 19)**, R 34 b 4.5 north-westward to R 28 c 2.1 and then in front of Mouquet Farm to R 33 a 7.7. All squares on map 19 are rectangle R. On the right of the line the 4th and 5th Canadian Mounted Rifles captured and held trenches leading to the Fabeck Graben where they set up blocks enabling them to provide enfilade fire to support the 2nd Division. On the left the 1st Canadian Mounted Rifles raided Mouquet Farm and a strong point nearby, point 73 where the Fabeck Graben crossed OG 1. The results of the 1st Canadian Mounted Rifles attack are reported in 8 Brigade War Diary:

> '*The raiding party on Mouquet Farm (Lt. French) was divided into two sections. One proceeded along the northern, and the other along the southern face. The northern party reached point 29 and proceeded along the German trench running toward point 12 where they bombed or bayoneted 50 or 60 Germans. This party then retired but lost heavily during retirement by rifle and machine gun fire from the Northwest. The southern party*

was forced to take shelter in the south-west corner of the farm where they remained and dug themselves in during the day. They were eventually relieved by a party of the 2nd Canadian Mounted Rifles after dark'.[6]

The fate of the party which attacked point 73 was reported at length by Brigadier-General J H Elmsley commanding 8 Canadian Infantry Brigade:

'At 6.20 a.m. Sept. 15th a party of four officers and 118 other ranks under Captain Caswell were in position in advance of their trench opposite point 73. The main body consisted of 50 men with the dug-outs at point 73 as their objective. Flanking parties of 25 men each were detailed with instructions to make an entry into the enemy trench on either flank of point 73 and from there to bomb inwards, as a protection to the main body.

At 6.20 a.m. our artillery commenced to shell this party heavily as they lay in the open ready to attack, the first two shells hitting about 25 yards in advance of point 91 forcing Captain Caswell to remove HQ to a new position to the left of this point. Whilst this was taking place the Germans manned the parapet of High Trench (Fabeck Graben) and brought enfilade fire to bear on our men in No Man's Land. The enemy also pushed out a bombing attack from point 73.

Our machine guns which had previously been posted on the flanks of point 91 brought effective fire to bear on High Trench and inflicted many casualties on the Germans manning the parapet. Captain Caswell, finding his position untenable, decided to move forward and attack the enemy. With this object in view he instructed his officer

The remains of a defensive emplacement in the ground to the north of Mouquet Farm.

THIEPVAL MEMORIAL

holding the trench immediately west of point 91 to advance. This officer, unfortunately, was killed before these instructions could be put into effect, and Captain Caswell found it impossible to move his party forward after he had lost all his officers and N.C.O.s

At about 8.25 a.m. our artillery lifted and this party was able to regain our original front line trench after having 60 killed or wounded, including 3 officers, out of the 118.

> 'Captain Caswell is positive that most of his casualties were
> inflicted by our artillery'. [7]

The 2nd Canadian Mounted Rifles were ordered 'to establish a strong point at Mouquet Farm and to consolidate the position by entrenching before handing over'. During 16 September they were heavily shelled but, when relieved at 4.45 a.m. the next morning, reported to the 5/Dorsets, 34th Brigade (11th Division) that the task had been accomplished and that Mouquet Farm was in British hands.

As part of the preparations for the forthcoming drive to capture Stuff and Zollern Redoubts to the north, towards Thiepval, the British 11th Division took over the line in front of Mouquet Farm from the Canadians. On the morning of 17 September 34 Brigade reported that Mouquet Farm was not captured and that the Canadian report that the trenches dug the previous day surrounded the farm was incorrect. The truth was that that the trench line ran through the farm which now consisted of three ruins. One of these was behind the British line and the other two in front of it. A tunnel connected all three and the Germans were using this to gain access to the rear of the British line. A deep-dug out was also known to exist under the ruin 40 yards in front of the brigade's line. The attack northwards took place on the 26 September and in the course of it Mouquet Farm finally fell. In the War Diary of 34 Brigade Second Lieutenant H. J. Ratcliffe gave a very full report on its capture:

> 'Mouquet Farm was known to hold about 50 Germans with
> at least one machine gun. In order to prevent this party
> interfering with the advance of the assaulting troops, a special
> bombing party was detailed from 9/Lancashire Fusiliers to rush
> all the entrances to the farm half a minute before the remainder
> of the troops were to leave the trenches.
>
> The party was completely successful in its mission and was
> relieved by a similar party from the 11/Manchesters under
> Lieutenant J Cooper who was killed shortly afterwards. To assist
> this operation of clearing the farm, two tanks allocated to the
> brigade were to pass the farm on their way to Zollern Road. They

both drove into a deep hole and remained stuck there for the next three days.

At 4.30 p.m. the occupants of the farm were causing many casualties so Lieutenant Dancer, 5/Dorsets, the officer of tank No 542 and its crew and Lieutenant Kohnstamm and six men of the 11/Manchesters and a sergeant and six men of the 6/East Yorkshire Pioneers lined the top of a mound on the building and placed two machine guns from the tanks to cover the Western and Northern entrances to the farm, while two bombing parties of the 11/Manchesters threw bombs down the entrances to the farm with no visible result. At 5.30 p.m. Lieutenant Low of 11/Manchesters threw smoke bombs down the entrances and shortly afterwards the occupants came out. One officer and fifty five other ranks. On examination, three machine guns, 2 flammenwerfers and two gas cylinders were found in the farm.

The actual taking of the farm cannot be claimed by any one unit as;

6/East Yorks., 11/Manchesters, 5/Dorsets and No 542 tank were all represented. The clearing of the farm was undoubtedly effected by the smoke bombs thrown by Lieutenant Lowe'. [8]

Author's note. The two spellings of Lieutenant Low(e)'s name appear in the original document.

Mouquet Farm: The German Perspective

Just as the Australians suffered under the almost continuous German bombardment, so the Germans found their trenches rendered almost untenable by the British bombardment. Only few troops were kept in the front line.

Following the loss of 5th Avenue (Ration Trench) to the 12th Division the II RI.R. and the III/157 I.R. holding 6th Avenue (Skyline Trench) were ordered to counter-attack to retake the lost trench. In this endeavour they were aided by one company of the 86th R.I.R. (9th Reserve Jäger Battalion) who, in spite of their inexperience, when they carried out a *Flammenwerfer* attack just after midnight on 8 August regained a substantial length of trench but, further west, the attack by the 157th and 11th failed. Fearing to be cut off, the commander of the 86th gave ground reducing his gain to about 150 yards. According to the British reports only 40 yards were lost.

When the new British barrage descended on the German lines in the afternoon of 8 August the effect in the recaptured stretch of 5th Avenue (Ration Trench) was so dramatic that by midnight the British were again in possession of that section of line. At the same time the

Australian 15th Battalion had attacked Park Lane, which was held by units of the 9th Reserve Jäger Battalion, the I/63rd I.R. on the left and the 6th Company 86th R.I.R. on the right. The German record shows that the I/63rd broke, leaving the centre unit vulnerable to attack from the rear and it, along with the 86th, were attacked and fell back allowing the Australians to capture their objective.

On 9 August General von Boehn, IX Reserve Corps, convinced that that the British were determined to succeed in their thrust towards Thiepval, put in a last request to the headquarters of the German Second Army for additional artillery for the Pozières sector, before

Staircases, which were under the rubble heaps of the main buildings of Mouquet Farm, descended to long galleries and dugouts running beneath the whole length of the courtyard. The dugouts, which could hold at least 200 men, constituted the strength of the position.

Mouquet Farm and the Quarry looking due north from Park Lane.
IWM E (AUS) 561

handing over to XIX Corps. The 16th Division took over the northern front immediately after the Australian attack of 8 August and the 24th Division took over to the east. The junction of the two divisions, in the firing line, was the point where the Courcelette track crossed O.G.1 and O.G.2. In the 16th Division area the 69th I.R. was directly opposite the Australians in front of Mouquet Farm with the 29th I.R. on their immediate right and the 28th I.R. on their far right. For the 24th Division the 133rd R.I.R. was next to the 16th Division with the 139th I.R. on their left as far as the main road and the 179th I.R. south of the road.

On 10 August the bombardment of the German lines around Mouquet Farm and 6th Avenue (Skyline Trench) was so severe that reports were sent by the 29th I.R. and the 69th I.R. that they were expecting to be attacked. The newly arrived divisions reacted to these concerns, the 24th brought up reserves and extra batteries of heavy howitzers were sited to drive the Australian 13th Battalion out of the sunken road between points 22 and 34 south-east of the farm. A heavy barrage was laid down on the north-western part of Pozières, 4th Avenue and Park Lane. Following the loss of ground on 11 August the 16th Division proposed a counter-attack, again with *Flammenwerfer*; while preparations were being made the 24th Division reported that it

The present day Mouquet Farm and the Quarry. Looking east from D73 April 1997.

MOUQUET FARM | THE QUARRY

was being attacked, north of the main road, and needed artillery support. The confusion engendered by this report resulted in a decision to hold the proposed counter-attack until a clearer picture was obtained. The German literature shows that they suffered in the same way as the Australians in being unsure of the exact positions of units and trenches and often mistook troop movements for full attacks. Bean suggests that tne attack reported by the 24th Division was nothing more than the Australian 50th Battalion relieving the 16th Battalion on 12 August. He goes on to state that later the same day:

> 'the 16th Division reported that it afterwards beat off an attack, and that thereupon, after intense bombardment, there followed another against the 29th and 69th Regiments. The British, it said, attacking the 29th forced their way into the north-eastern part of Skyline Trench, but the 69th reported that the attempt in its sector (i.e. that of the 50th and 13th Australian Battalions) failed'. [9]

Following the capture of 6th Avenue (Skyline Trench) by the British II Corps the commander of XIX Corps ordered its immediate recapture. An artillery barrage involving every available unit blasted 6th Avenue and at 10.30 p.m. a counter-attack was launched lead by the II/68th which captured the trench up to point 81 just before midnight. The Germans had been lead to believe that the enemy had retired under the

The 'Harvest' at Mouquet Farm April 1997.

The village as it was some months after the battle. The view is from the southern side of the main road looking southwards, east of the "Copse." The grave, which was subsequently lost, is that of Captain I.S. Margetts, 12th Battalion. His name is recorded on the Villers-Bretonneux Memorial.

artillery barrage but when the trench was taken it was found to be full of British dead.

By 14 August the Germans were convinced that a major attack on Mouquet Farm was imminent. Orders were given that, should a breakthrough be gained on either side of the farm, an immediate counter-attack must be made by the 16th Division using all available reserves. The 24th Division would also attack on the Australian flank. As a consequence of this order the headquarters was flooded with more erroneous reports of major attacks. When on 18 August Walker launched his twin attacks which lead to the capture of point 55 the German 16th Division put all its reserves into the line and reported, after the battle, that further defensive operations were beyond its resources. In response the 15th R.I.R. (2nd Guard Reserve Division), newly arrived on the battlefield, was put under the orders of the 16th Division.

The Australian attacks of 20/21 August were directed at the 16th Division. According to Bean:

> 'On the German side.....at Mouquet Farm an advance between the farm and the sunken road was admitted. The front appears to have been held by the 1/69th brought back to the line for the third time within a fortnight'. [10]

Before the Australian 21st Battalion attack on 26 August XIX Corps was relieved the 16th Division and part of the 24th were replaced by the Guard Reserve Corps. Its 4th Guard Division took over the line from Thiepval to Point 54 (north-west of Mouquet Farm) and the 1st Guard Reserve Division, Mouquet Farm and that part of the 24th Division line facing I Anzac.

In common with the divisions leaving the line, the Guard Reserve Division, fearful of the power of the Australian assaults, set up a continuous barrage in front of the farm and planned a counter-attack on the line from point 4 to the main road. The proposed date for this attack was 5 September, but these preparations were upset by further Australian action on 29 August. In this they failed to take point 54, held by the 5th Guard Grenadier Regiment while the remainder of the attack, falling upon the 2nd Guard Reserve Regiment, initially won the farm but was subsequently driven back by counter action.

On 3 September another successful counter-attack was made by III/Ist Guard Reserve Regiment from the north-east and north together with the II/64th from the west. Although ground was retaken the losses sustained by the Germans were so great that they feared that any subsequent Australian attack would be unstoppable. The proposed counter-attack on the 5 September did not take place and on that day the 1st Guard Reserve Division began to be relieved by the 45th Reserve Division, to be followed by the 4th Guard Division on 12 September.

Bibliography

1. *The Official History of Australia in the War 1914-1918.* Volume III. Bean. 1929.
2. Ibid.
3. *Military Operations in France & Belgium. 1916* Volume II. Miles. Macmillan 1938.
4. *The Fifth Army* General Sir Hubert Gough. Hodder & Stoughton 1931.
5. *Military Operations in France & Belgium.* 1916 Volume II. Miles. Macmillan 1938
6. War Diary Canadian 8 Infantry Brigade. Public Record Office. WO 95/3868
7. Ibid.
8. War Diary 34 Infantry Brigade. Public Record Office. WO 951818.
9. *The Official History of Australia in the War 1914-1918.* Volume III. Bean. 1929.
10. Ibid.

Chapter Five

LIEUTENANT BUTTERWORTH AND
CAPTAIN JACKA

George Sainton Kaye Butterworth MC 1885-1916

At 9.25 p.m. on 27 July 1916 the 13/Durham Light Infantry, 68 Brigade, 23rd Division relieved the 10/Northumberland Fusiliers in the vicinity of Munster Alley **(See map 20)**. The right flank was at Martinpuich road, point 72 (Three Trees), the centre between Sussex Trench and point 22 (the junction of Gloster Alley and OG 2) and the left on point 78. In addition, the company on the extreme left had its headquarters in the bombing post, point 41, at the junction of Munster Alley and OG 2.

The War Diary of the 13/Durham Light Infantry for that day states:

> *'At 10 p.m. Lieutenant Butterworth, A Company and one company of the 12th Battalion Durham Light Infantry commenced a trench from X.6.C.8.6 in a north-westerly direction and parallel with the German Switch Line running from S.1.C.2.9 to Munster Alley. By 3.00 a.m. the trench had been dug for 200 yards and was held by two platoons of A company. Lieutenant G.S. Kay-Butterworth was wounded on duty'.*[1]

On 28 July the battalion was relieved by the 10/West Riding Regiment but returned to the front line on 2 August. From then on the War Diary refers to the trench above as Butterworth Trench, as do all subsequent official maps. During the night of 2/3 August parties of the 13/Durham Light Infantry augmented by the 10/Northumberland Fusiliers, carried out work widening and deepening Butterworth Trench and Gloster Alley and repaired a gap in OG 1. Again relieved at 6.20 a.m. on 3 August they moved to billets near Contalmaison, but returned at 3.00 p.m. on 4 August in preparation for an attack on Munster Alley and Torr Trench in accordance with 68 Brigade Operation Order No 74.[2]

The artillery carried out an intense bombardment at 1.00 a.m. and again at 6.00 a.m. At 7.00 p.m. a continuous bombardment of the enemy lines was started and continued until 9.15 p.m., when two minutes intense bombardment was started. At 9.16 p.m. Torr Trench was attacked by D Company, but it was immediately hit by rifle and machine gun fire from Torr Trench and Munster Alley. They managed to cross Munster Alley, but only a few men of the second wave entered Torr Trench where a bombing fight ensued which continued until about 2.15 a.m. After the second wave crossed Munster Alley a

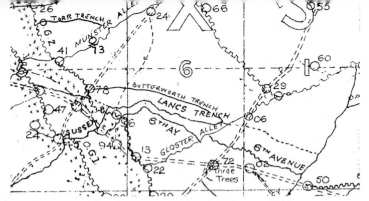

Map 20. Trench Map, Butterworth Trench, 4 August 1916.

bombing party from B Company and the remnants of D Company, moved up Munster Alley until stopped at about 60 yards by a heavily wired barricade supported by a machine gun 40 yards south-west of point 73. They set up their own block some yards back from the enemy. Further attacks on Torr Trench being thought unlikely to succeed, the company commander, Captain G. White, decided to concentrate on gaining ground in Munster Alley. As the night progressed further reinforcements were sent forward to break the enemy's block but all failed and at about 9.00 a.m. the bombing and counter-bombing finally ceased.

At 12.00 a.m. Lieutenant Butterworth, with A Company, was ordered to proceed as quickly as possible from his position in Butterworth Trench, to take part in the action in Munster Alley. He was unable to carry out this order as almost at once he came under 'friendly' artillery fire. At 3.41 a.m. he managed to reach the Alley but at 4.45 a.m. was reported killed. The attack on Torr Trench failed but some progress was made in Munster Alley.

George Butterworth was born in London on 13 July 1885. He spent most of his childhood in York, where his father was general manager of the North Eastern Railway. From preparatory school at Aysgarth he went to Eton and, in 1904, to Trinity College Oxford. Already a musician before going to Oxford, he became president of the University Music Club. On leaving the University he was offered, and accepted, a post as music master at Radley. He did so in order to support himself, which he considered impossible by means of musical composition alone. He remained at Radley for two years before enrolling as a student at the Royal College of Music, where he studied for about a year under Sir Hubert Parry and Dr Charles Wood.

Folk music was to play a large part in Butterworth's life, encouraged by his great friend Ralph Vaughan Willams. He joined the Folk Music Society in 1906 and took part in Morris Dancing. In 1911 and 1912 he published two sets of songs from A.E. Houseman's *Shropshire Lad* and in 1913 the rhapsody - perhaps his best known work -*A Shropshire Lad* was performed at the Leeds Festival, to be followed in March 1914 by *The Banks Of Green Willow.*

When war broke out, Butterworth was in Stratford-on-Avon in connection with his membership of the English Folk Dance Society. After failing to be recommended by the Oxford University OTC, he succeeded in joining the 6/Duke of Cornwall's Light Infantry on 1 September 1914. Rejecting any thought of a commission he, and a group of friends with whom he had enlisted, commenced training at Bodmin, but later moved to Aldershot. In November, he was finally persuaded to accept a commission on the understanding that he would do so only if all his friends were similarly treated. There by now being no vacancies for officers in the Duke of Cornwall's Light Infantry, he transferred to the 13/Durham Light Infantry at Bullswater Camp with the rank of Second Lieutenant. Promoted Lieutenant in May 1915, he finally entered the trenches on 10 September at Sailly-sur-Lys. In June 1916 he moved to the Somme and for his action at Contalmaison on 27 July was recommended for the MC.

Brigadier-General Page Croft commanding 68 Infantry Brigade, writing of the attack on Torr Trench and Munster Alley says:

> *'Before light I went up the line to find out the exact situation........I went up to the farthest point reached by Lieutenant Kaye-Butterworth. The trench was very low and broken, and he kept urging me to keep low down. I had only reached the battalion headquarters on my return when I heard poor Butterworth, a brilliant musician in times of peace, and an equally brilliant soldier in times of stress, was shot dead by a bullet through the head. So he who had been so thoughtful for my safety had suffered the fate he had warned me against only a minute before'.* [3]

Ironically the notification of his award of the MC was included in battalion orders for the day following his death.

Butterworth has no known grave, but is listed on the Thiepval Memorial under the name Kaye-Butterworth, by which name he is also listed in Officers Died in the Great War.

Albert Jacka VC MC 1893-1932

Albert Jacka was born at Winchelsea, Victoria on 10 January 1893, the fourth child and second son of Nathaniel and Elizabeth Jacka. He enlisted in Melbourne on 8

September 1914 and was assigned to the 14th Battalion 4 Brigade. The battalion, under Lieutenant-Colonel R.E. Courtney, left Melbourne on 22 December and arrived in Alexandria on 30 January 1915. After a period of training in Egypt the battalion sailed for Gallipoli, arriving at Mudros harbour (Lemos) on 15 April as part of the Anzac force commanded by Lieutenant-General W.R. Birdwood. 4 Brigade was in reserve and left Mudros at 10 a.m. on Sunday 25 April to land on the peninsula at 10.30 a.m. the following day, although Jacka landed in the evening of the 25th as part of an advanced party. The battalion was ordered to an exposed position which became known as Courtney's Post.

On 19 May the Turks launched a major attack on trenches on the ridge bearing Courtney's Post. At 3.30 a.m. they entered one bay of a trench, but were unable to move either north or south by Australians still holding the line. Jacka was in a sap opposite a communication trench running across the northern end of the captured trench. Aided by two comrades, he leapt into the captured trench and fired at the Turks, but was forced to retire when the other two Australians were killed. He made his way behind the captured trench to the other end and attacked again, jumping into the trench, shooting five Turks and bayoneting two more. The remainder fled back over the parapet. For this action Jacka was awarded the Victoria Cross, the first to be won by the AIF in the Great War, which was presented to him by King George V at Buckingham Palace on 29 September 1916. Bean quotes Lieutenant G.W. Crabbe, the first officer to enter the trench after Jacka's action:

> 'On entering the position which was piled high with dead of both sides, Crabbe found Jacka with an unlighted cigarette in his mouth and flushed with the excitement of the preceding hour. "I managed to get the beggars, Sir," he said.'[4]

The Australian Prime Minister, William Hughes, who saw Jacka as a means to bolster recruitment, allowed his friend, the newspaperman Keith Murdoch, to use Jacka's name in support of a campaign without Jacka's permission.

By the time the 14th Battalion left Gallipoli in December 1915, Jacka had been promoted to the rank of Company Sergeant Major. Following a short stop at Lemnos, the battalion sailed back to Alexandria where, in common with other units, it underwent a reorganisation. A new battalion was created and new officers were required. Jacka was selected and gazetted Second Lieutenant on 29 April 1916 and promoted Lieutenant on 18 August 1916.

With the battalion he sailed to France, landed at Marseilles and entrained on 8 June for the long journey to Bailleul. The 4th Division entered the Somme campaign on 6 August and on the 7th Jacka was involved with the incident at the Elbow. Newton Wanless, the historian of the 14th Battalion wrote:

'It was a marvellous piece of work, bold in conception, brilliant and heroic in execution, smashing and demoralising to the enemy, and fruitful in its results a splendid piece of bluff carried to a successful and glorious conclusion by a handful of men who had already endured a nerve-racking bombardment of several hours. The records of the AIF teem with successful exploits in the face of great odds, but they do not contain anything which surpasses (if anything quite equals) the work of Jacka and his seven on Pozières Ridge'.[5]

In a footnote Wanless states that there was a strong feeling within the battalion that the action merited a second VC. In the event Jacka was awarded an MC, which was consistent with the report sent up to Brigade by Lieutenant-Colonel C.M. Dare. It is also of interest that no mention of the deed appears in the Battalion War Diary for that day. [6] Much has been made of Jacka's relations with his superiors, which were never good. He always had confidence in his own judgement and ability but was often scornful of superiors and at times did not fail to let his opinion be known to them. In part, at least, this may explain why further decorations were refused, along with promotion above the rank of captain.

Jacka was wounded seven times in the fight on the ridge with one bullet going straight through his chest and out of his back. Sent first to hospital in France and then London, he was not fit to rejoin the battalion until November 1916. By January 1917 the new battalion commanding officer, Lieutenant-Colonel John Peck, had secured Jacka's promotion to captain and appointed him to the job of battalion intelligence officer.

The AIF, already less than impressed by British generalship, was to

View of Brind's Road and ground between the track to Courcelette and the north side of Pozières village. AERIAL PHOTOGRAPH TREVOR PIDGEON

COURCELETTE

D'S ROAD

O G LINES

POZIÈRES CEMETERY

MOUQUET FARM

become further disenchanted in April at Bullecourt. Before the action, Jacka, as intelligence officer, went forward, at night into No Man's Land and found an unoccupied stretch of sunken road. This road, about 350 yards ahead of the Australian position, provided an ideal jumping off point for the attack. For this and subsequent work during the action Jacka gained a bar to his MC. The attack was to be lead by tanks which failed to arrive at the scheduled hour and the troops, already well out in the snow in No Man's Land, had to be brought back. On the following night the same men were sent out but this time the tanks came early. With no sound cover from artillery, the Germans heard their approach and were alerted to the attack. The tanks were too slow to cross No Man's Land in front of the infantry in the time allowed and the Australian soldiers found themselves held up by uncut wire and were decimated.

In the reorganisation which followed Jacka was passed over for promotion and lost his post as intelligence officer, returning to take charge of D Company. In June at Messines he once more took a leading role and was again wounded, this time in the leg by a sniper. Hospitalised in England, he did not return to the front until shortly before Polygon Wood in late September where he again did well. On 15 May he was seriously gassed just north of Villers-Bretonneux. The effects were so serious that when he was finally discharged from hospital he was only fit for light duties. His war was over!

Returning to Australia in October 1919 he was given a civic welcome in Melbourne in the presence of the governor-general, followed towards the end of the month, by a smaller local event at Wedderburn. He was demobilised in January 1920 and went into business selling electrical items. As the business prospered he moved into local politics and worked for the benefit of old soldiers. With the coming of the depression his business failed but, as Mayor of St Kilda, he continued to do his best for the unemployed but died in January 1932. At his funeral his coffin was carried by eight VC holders. It is debatable whether he ever really fitted into civilian life after his experiences in the war.

Bibliography
1. War Diary 13th Battalion Durham Light Infantry. Public Record Office. WO 95/2182.
2. War Diary 68 Infantry Brigade. Public Record Office. WO 95/2181.
3. *Twenty-Two Months under Fire.* Page Croft. 1917.
4. *The Official History of Australia in the War 1914-1918.* Volume III. Bean. 1929.
5. *The History of the Fourteenth Battalion AIF.* Wanless. 1929.
6. War Diary 14th Infantry Battalion. AIF. Public Record Office. WO 95/3494.

Chapter Six

SEVEN VICTORIA CROSSES

The Victoria Cross was founded by Royal Warrant on 29 January 1856. Originally awarded to men of the army and navy the warrant has been amended several times and now allows for the award to be made to other categories of recipient. The Maltese cross is still made of bronze from cannon captured during the Crimean War and carries the inscription 'For Valour'. In the fighting for Pozières and Mouquet Farm between 23 July and 9 September 1916 seven Victoria Crosses were won; of these, five went to Australia, one to Canada and one to Great Britain. The approximate positions of each of the recipients are shown on **map 21**.

Private John Leak 9th Australian Infantry Battalion A.I.F.

On 23 July the 9th Battalion 3 Brigade was on the extreme right of the Australian line. When the attack went in the battalion made ground, but was eventually held up by strong resistance in the OG Lines, particularly near the junction of OG 1 with Pozières Trench. Slightly in advance of this junction was a strong point where a communication trench entered OG 1 from Munster Alley. Enemy bombers using 'egg' bombs were able to out-distance the Australians until Private Leak ran forward over open ground to throw three bombs into the strong point. As the smoke cleared he jumped into the trench and bayoneted the remaining Germans. For this action he was awarded the Victoria Cross.

John Leak was born in Portsmouth in 1892 and emigrated to Australia, where he worked in Queensland as a teamster. He enlisted in 1915 and served in Gallipoli before going to France. On 21 August, during the fighting for Mouquet Farm, he was wounded but after treatment returned to his unit until in March 1918 when he was again wounded, being severely gassed at Hollebeke. He returned to Australia when the war ended, married and subsequently ran a garage business in Western Australia. He retired to Crafters, South Australia, where he died on 20 October 1972.

Lieutenant Arthur S Blackburn   10th Australian Infantry Battalion A.I.F.

On the same day and in almost the same place as John Leak, Arthur Blackburn also won the Victoria Cross. The 10th Battalion were in support to the 9th Battalion and at 5.30 a.m. Lieutenant Blackburn and 50 men of D Company were sent forward. A Company had already suffered heavily in trying to aid the 9th Battalion and were pinned down. The battalion historian C.B.L. Lock records what followed:

'On arrival he found that A Company 10th Battalion was suffering heavy casualties from bombs and machine guns. He at once rushed the barricade, breaking it down and bombing the enemy back. The artillery bombardment had almost obliterated the trench and reduced it to a scene of shell craters which made our advance more difficult, because advancing troops were exposed to the enemy's heavy machine gun fire. The enemy very stubbornly held his position and stopped for a time our advance. Lieutenant Blackburn, accompanied by four men, crawled forward to ascertain if possible where the machine gun fire was coming from. The four men who accompanied him were killed, and he had to return to his platoon'.

Under cover of mortar fire Blackburn went out a second time in search of the machine gun but again was forced to retire. Now an artillery barrage was laid down and he made a third attempt, advancing thirty yards before being stopped by enemy bombers.

'His bomber then engaged the enemy and under this cover Lieutenant Blackburn and Sergeant Inwood crawled forward to reconnoitre the position. They ascertained that the enemy held a trench which cut the one they were attacking at right angles. Lieutenant Blackburn therefore decided to clear this trench and succeeded in doing so. The trench was about 120 yards long, and was blind. The trench was consolidated, and after considerable trouble, communication with the 9th Battalion troops on the left was established. During the work of consolidation, Sergeant Inwood - who had done splendidly - and three men were killed'.[1]

Robert Inwood was one of three brothers who served in the A.I.F. Reginald was awarded the Victoria Cross at Polygon Wood in September 1917. The third brother, Harold, was wounded in France and returned to Australia in November 1917.

Blackburn held the trench until relieved at 2.00 p.m. He was recommended for the Victoria Cross by Lieutenant-Colonel S.P. Weir.

Arthur Blackburn was born in Woodville (South Australia) in 1892, the son of the rector of St Margaret's Woodville. In 1914, already a qualified lawyer, he enlisted and took part in the Anzac landing in Gallipoli. He was commissioned Second Lieutenant in August and promoted full Lieutenant in February 1916. In the September following Pozières he became sick and was evacuated to hospital in London. Here he was invested with the Victoria Cross by King George V. His health was now too poor for further service and he returned to Australia in December 1916 to resume his legal profession.

In 1925 he returned to the military and by 1939 was Lieutenant-Colonel commanding the 18th Light Horse (Machine Gun) Regiment. In the Second World War he saw service in Syria and Java, where he was captured by the Japanese. After the war he worked as a Commonwealth Conciliation Commissioner. He died suddenly in November 1960.

Private Thomas Cooke 8th Australian Infantry Battalion A.I.F.

On 24 July the 8th Infantry Battalion was given the task of moving up through Pozières village, the battalion War Diary describes the action as follows:

'At 0330 under cover of artillery fire the attack was launched, the battalion attacking on a frontage of two companies ("C" and "D" Coys) right and left respectively with "B" Company in support. The attack proceeded vigorously through the village, each trench and strong-post being quickly cleared of the enemy. The left company "D" with an irresistible advance reached its objective by 5 a.m. and proceeded to establish itself 50 yards north of the cemetery. Our right company "C" met with strong opposition, but fighting with great determination speedily overcame it, and shortly after 5 a.m., reached their objective

Pozières cemetery September 1916. IWM E(AUS) 1

North East of the village and at once dug in. Bombing parties of 4th Battalion working up a German trench co-operated splendidly, driving the enemy towards a position occupied by our left company, where they were either killed or made prisoner'.[2]

During this action a Lewis gun became disabled and Cooke was ordered to take his gun and gun-team to what the citation in the London Gazette described as, 'a dangerous part of the line'. His team was gradually killed until he alone remained, continuing to fire until he too was hit. For his 'determination and devotion to duty' Cooke was posthumously awarded the Victoria Cross. Despite counter-attacks and heavy artillery bombardment the 8th Battalion managed to hold their ground until relieved at 3 a.m. on 27 July.

Thomas Cooke was born in New Zealand in 1881. He married in 1902 and with his wife and three children moved to Melbourne Australia in 1912. He enlisted in 1915 in the 24th Infantry Battalion but later transferred to the 8th Battalion. He has no known grave but is commemorated on the Australian Memorial at Villers-Bretonneux.

Sergeant Claud C. Castleton 5th Australian Machine Gun Company A.I.F.

As part of the ill-fated attack on the OG Lines by the Australian 2nd Division on 28 July 5 Brigade were ordered to attack between the main road and Munster Alley. Poor preparation lead to the enemy detecting the troops as they moved into open ground prior to zero hour. The men of the 20th Battalion had already been spotted as they formed up near the railway line. The enemy immediately opened fire with machine guns and a barrage of high explosive and gas. No advance was possible and men who had moved forward had to remain in the open for some three hours before withdrawal was practical. In the interim Sergeant Castleton went out into No Man's Land on two occasions and brought in a wounded man on his back. On his third foray he was himself hit in the back and killed. For his 'courage and self-sacrifice' he was posthumously awarded the Victoria Cross.

Claud Castleton was born in South Lowestoft Suffolk in 1893. He moved to Australia in 1912, where he travelled widely in Victoria, New South Wales, Queensland and Tasmania. In March 1915 he enlisted in the A.I.F. in Sydney. He went to Gallipoli and, following the evacuation, continued to serve with the 18th Battalion. The following month he transferred to the 5th Machine Gun Company and was confirmed in the rank of sergeant. He is buried in Pozières British Cemetery.

Private Martin O'Meara 16th Australian Infantry Battalion A.I.F.

On 11 August the 16th Battalion attacked point 61 which was situated south-east of the Quarry and adjacent to the point where Park Lane cut the track running between Mouquet Farm and Brind's Road. Finding the point almost obliterated, they proceeded to dig a communication trench to link up with K Trench. This was completed before dawn, at which time the battalion was subjected to a heavy bombardment which went on until midday. In the afternoon the Germans launched a counter-attack from Mouquet Farm which was repulsed with the aid of fire from the 13th Battalion. As the enemy retired or sought shelter they, in turn, were pounded by intense artillery fire.

During this episode and over a total of four days O'Meara, a stretcher-bearer, repeatedly went out into No Man's Land to bring in wounded. As recorded in the citation in the London Gazette, 'He also volunteered and carried up ammunition and bombs through a heavy barrage to a portion of the trenches which was being heavily shelled at the time. He showed thorough contempt for danger and undoubtedly saved many lives'.

Martin O'Meara was born in County Tipperary in 1885. The exact date of his move to Australia is not known, but he lived in South Australia before going to Western Australia, where he enlisted. He served in Gallipoli and remained in the 16th Battalion for the whole of the war, achieving the rank of sergeant by 1918. He was wounded three times, once in 1916 and twice the following year. After the war his health failed and he spent the next seventeen years in military hospitals. On his death he was buried in Perth with full military honours.

Private William Short 8th Battalion The Green Howards.

Following the failure of the 13/Durham Light Infantry to capture Torr Trench on 4 August, another attempt was made the following day by the 8/Green Howards, 69 Brigade, 23rd Division. The earlier attack had resulted in the capture of about sixty yards of Munster Alley and the Green Howards managed to bomb the enemy from a further 150 yards and gained a footing in what remained of Torr Trench. The ground in the vicinity of Torr Trench had been pounded by the artillery to such good effect that the trench had almost ceased to exist. It was during this fight that Private Short won his Victoria Cross, the third awarded to the Green Howards on the Somme.

Short was a bomber and although wounded in the foot refused to go for treatment, preferring to stay and fight with his mates. He was wounded again by a shell, this time his whole leg was shattered, but still he continued preparing bombs from a position at the bottom of a trench. The fight went on for about five hours and although relieved and offered medical attention Short was too seriously wounded to survive. His award was a posthumous one.

William Short was born in Eston, Middlesbrough in 1887. Before the war he was employed in the local steelworks and was a well known footballer. He enlisted in 1914 and had served with the 23rd

The Grave of Private W Short VC. Contalmaison Chateau Cemetery.

Division since it went to France in August 1915. He is buried in Contalmaison Chateau Cemetery.

Corporal Leo Clarke 2nd Battalion Eastern Ontario Regiment C.E.F.

 By early September 1st Canadian Division had started to replace the Australians. At 4.45 p.m. on 9 September the 2nd Canadian Battalion (1 Brigade 1st Canadian Division) attacked the enemy trenches astride the railway leading to Martinpuich south of the Albert-Bapaume road. They succeeded in capturing about 500 yards of trench but were counter-attacked and bombarded by the German artillery. Corporal Clarke was ordered to take a bombing party to clear part of the left flank and then to cover the construction of a trench block. Most of the bombers became casualties and, while building a temporary barricade, Clarke was counter-attacked by about twenty German soldiers led by two officers. He managed to fight them off using only his revolver and two captured enemy rifles. One of the German officers attacked Clarke with a bayonet and wounded him severely in the leg before himself being shot. The remaining Germans retreated, pursued by Clarke, who killed four more and captured a fifth. The block was completed and Clarke sent to the dressing station. He returned to the line next day but the wounds deteriorated and he was sent to hospital at Etretat where he died on 19 October, a week before the award of the Victoria cross was gazetted.

Leo Clarke was born in Hamilton Ontario in 1892. He spent part of his childhood in England, his parents returning to Canada in or around 1904. He enlisted in February 1915 in the 27th Battalion but later, wishing to be with his brother, transferred to the 2nd Battalion. He is buried in Etretat Churchyard, Le Havre.

Bibliography
1. *History of the 10th Battalion AIF.* Lock.
2. War Diary 8th Infantry Battalion AIF. Public Record Office. WO 95/3611.

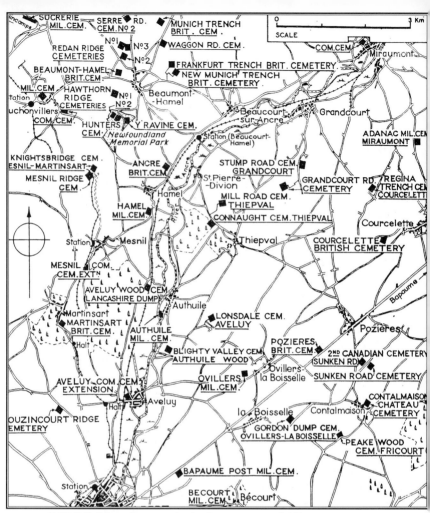

C.W.G.C. Map of cemeteries in the area around Albert.

Burial of a soldier in Bécourt Cemetery, August 1916. The burial party consists of British and Australian troops.

Chapter Seven

CEMETERIES AND MEMORIALS

Introduction

What Rudyard Kipling called 'The Silent Cities' stand as testament to the deeds and sacrifice of all those who fought and died for 'King and Country'. The cemeteries on the Western Front, constructed in the period following the Armistice, on ground 'given in perpetuity' by France and Belgium, are havens of peace in what were once areas of unimaginable horror. All, except for the very smallest, contain a Cross of Sacrifice designed by Sir Reginald Blomfield. There are four sizes of cross, the one used depending upon the number of burials. Each cross carries a bronze sword pointing downwards, the meaning of which is open to individual interpretation. In cemeteries containing in excess of 400 graves a 'Stone of Remembrance' is also to be found. Designed by Sir Edwin Lutyens, it is usually a monolith, the dimensions of which to quote Lutyens himself are such that:

'All horizontal surfaces and planes are spherical and parts of parallel spheres, 1801 feet, 8 inches in diameter, and all its vertical lines converging upwards to a point some 1801 feet, 8 inches, above the centre of the spheres.'

The upkeep of the cemeteries is the responsibility of the Commonwealth War Graves Commission. They provide registers to all cemeteries, although some smaller ones are grouped together. It is unfortunate that in certain places these registers are constantly having to be replaced. It is difficult to understand how anyone sufficiently interested to visit a war cemetery can be so selfish as to remove the register.

The number of cemeteries in the vicinity of Pozières is quite large. Some have been described in other volumes in this series but, since none is exclusive to a particular action, some overlap is inevitable. The Commonwealth War Graves Commission map shows the positions of cemeteries and exact locations are given with each individual entry. Visitors may not be aware that the commission has available three overprinted Michelin maps which show the locations of all cemeteries in France and Belgium. These are available from their offices in Maidenhead, price £3 each.

111

Courcelette British Cemetery

Courcelette cemetery is about half a mile south-west of Courcelette Village. It is best reached from the D929 Albert-Bapaume road by taking the D107 to Courcelette and following the distinctive green Commonwealth War Graves Commission sign from the village. Following the fighting for Pozières and Mouquet Farm, Courcelette was captured by the Canadians on 15th September 1916. The cemetery was started in 1916 under the name 'Mouquet Road' or 'Sunken Road' and enlarged after the Armistice by concentration from smaller nearby cemeteries: Mouquet Farm,which was to the north of the farm and Red Chateau, which was in the village of Courcelette.

The register records the particulars of 1956 burials, mainly United Kingdom and Australian, of which 1177 are unknown. There are five special memorials.

As you approach from the village you turn right on to a track running past the cemetery. The track you are on is the one referred to as the 'Courcelette Track' in the Official History, which joined Brind's Road between Pozières cemetery and Mouquet Farm. In 1916 the track running in front of the cemetery ran all the way to Mouquet Farm but now stops well short. The major German trench, the Fabeck Graben, ran from behind the farm and along the track to a point close to the British cemetery.

Among the Australians buried here is Lieutenant Leander de Lorme Grove who was killed in the attack by the 49th battalion at Mouquet Farm on 3 September 1916. Like many of the Australians he was born in the United Kingdom, at Leyton. He lies in Plot IX Row G 5.

Another interesting grave is that of Lieutenant J C Mewburn, 18th Battalion Canadian Infantry, killed on 15 September 1916. He was the son of Major-General S C Mewburn C.M.G., Minister of Militia and Defence in the Canadian Government.This grave is in fact a special memorial located at the end of Plot I Row A.

Lieutenant John Chilton Mewbu... **Courcelette Cemetery.**

Pozières British Cemetery and Memorial

The Cemetery and Memorial is situated on the north-west side of the Albert-Bapaume road D929, just before it reaches Pozières. In 1916 the position appeared as point 66 on trench maps but was also known as 'Red Cross Corner' or 'Tramway Crossing'. The original plot started in 1916 is now Plot 2. The remaining burials were as a result of concentration after the Armistice from nearby smaller cemeteries, particularly Casualty Corner (Contalmaison), Danube Post (between Thiepval village and Mouquet Farm) and Nab Junction (Ovillers). The majority of these were 1916 casualties but some date from the 1918 offensive.

The cemetery now contains 2730 graves (1807 United Kingdom, 714 Australian and 209 Canadian) and of these 1353 are unknown. There are 21 special memorials.

Sergeant C Castleton VC. Pozieres Cemetery.

The memorial panels surrounding the cemetery record the names of the fallen with no known graves from the Fifth Army in 1918. For visitors unfamiliar with the layout of memorial panels, trying to find a particular name can be quite a daunting task. The panels are arranged by regiments following the order of precedence starting on the left hand side. If searching for one of the numerous infantry units I recommend the 'crib' produced by Ronald Clifton, Historical Information Officer of the Western Front Association, in *'Stand To'* No 49, April 1997.

Many of the Australian graves in Pozières cemetery do not record the exact date of death reflecting, no doubt, the confusion that reigned. One such is that of Private Charles Taylor, 1st Battalion Australian Infantry, killed in action 22nd/25th July. His grave is in Plot IV Row P 8.

Sergeant Claud Castleton, Australian Machine

Pozières British Cemetery and Memorial circa 1920.

Gun Corps, who was posthumously awarded the Victoria Cross, is buried in Plot IV Row L 43. The cemetery register contains an extract from the London Gazette dated 26 September 1916 recording his courage and self-sacrifice.

In Plot I Row H 42 lies Lieutenant Charles Clarebrough, 21st Infantry Battalion, who was killed in the action on 26 August near ZigZag Trench.

Sunken Road Cemetery & 2nd Canadian Cemetery Sunken Road.

These two small cemeteries are well worth a visit particularly if you decide to follow walk No 2 which takes you past them. The sunken road in their names is the one which runs from the D73 Pozières-Bazentin road in a south-westerly direction to join the D147 Pozières-Contalmaison road. The top part of this track, running through the Vallèe de Bois Derrieux, was the front line for the Australians in their attack on 23 July. The two cemeteries were made in July-October 1916. The registers record particulars of 214 war graves in Sunken Road and 44 in 2nd Canadian. There are also five special memorials in Sunken Road Cemetery.

Ovillers Military Cemetery

This is the largest cemetery in the area and is situated on the right hand side of the road running from Ovillers to Aveluy. The register states that it was begun before the capture of Ovillers (17 July) as a battle cemetery behind a dressing station and used until March 1917. These burials now make up about half of Plot 1. After the Armistice the size of the cemetery was increased by the concentration of graves from the surrounding battlefields and from at least two smaller cemeteries, Mash Valley and Red Dragon. As the name suggests, the latter was started by men of 38th Welsh Division and the burials were almost all Royal Welsh Fusiliers.

It now contains 3436 graves (3265 United Kingdom, 95 Canadian , 57 Australian, 13 South African and 6 New Zealand). Of these a very high proportion, 2477 are unidentified. There are 23 special memorials. In addition, there is a large French plot.

Ovillers cemetery contains a number of graves from the attacks in early July. Lieutenant-Colonel L M Howard, 24th (Tyneside Irish) Battalion Northumberland Fusiliers, who died near the Lochnagar crater on 2 July lies in Plot II Row D 4. Lieutenant-Colonel F C Heneker, Leinster Regiment, commanding the 21st (Tyneside Scottish) Battalion of the same regiment lies in Plot III Row A 1. He was killed

114

on the previous day.

Also to be found in Ovillers is Private F Barnes, Buckinghamshire Battalion Ox & Bucks Light Infantry, who was killed on 23 July in the 48th Division attack. He lies in Plot XI Row J 10.

Contalmaison Chateau Cemetery

Contalmaison Chateau Cemetery is in Contalmaison village and well signposted. To gain access you must walk up a short path running beside a garden. It was begun in mid July 1916 in the grounds of the chateau and used until March 1917 by Field Ambulances and again for a few burials in 1918. Only 47 graves were added after the Armistice so that the cemetery is quite small. It contains 289 graves (264 United Kingdom, 21 Australian and 4 Canadians). There are 45 unknown graves and one special memorial.

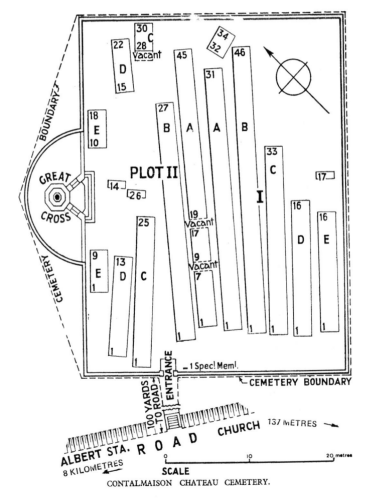

CONTALMAISON CHATEAU CEMETERY.

The chateau was not rebuilt after the war.

This cemetery contains the grave of another Victoria Cross holder, Private William Short. Short served in "C" Company, 8th Battalion Green Howards. At the time of the award the regiment was still officially known as the Yorkshire Regiment and it is this name which appears on the headstone. The name was changed in 1921. In common with other holders of the Victoria Cross the headstone carries the design of the cross and the cemetery register contains an extract from the London Gazette recording the deed for which the award was made. The grave is in Plot II Row B 16.

Villers-Bretonneux Memorial

No tour of the Somme battlefield, especially one following an Australian action, is complete without a visit to the Australian National Memorial at Villers-Bretonneux.

Dedicated to the Australian soldiers who fought in France and Belgium, to their dead, and especially to those of the dead whose graves are unknown, it is situated to the east of Amiens on the D23 road between Villers-Bretonneux and Fouilloy. Designed by Sir Edwin Lutyens it stands behind the cemetery and is in the form of a bell-tower 100 feet high with flanking walls. The Memorial Panels, beneath the tower, carry in excess of 10,000 names, many from the Pozières and Mouquet Farm fighting. The panel for the 8th Battalion contains the name of Private Thomas Cooke who was posthumously awarded the Victoria Cross for his action on 26 July. The letters VC appear before his name.

The cemetery was made after the Armistice and contains the graves of 1089 soldiers from the United Kingdom, 779 from Australia, 267 from Canada, 4 from South Africa and 2 from New Zealand. Of these 607 are unknown and there are 4 special memorials.

MEMORIALS

There are five memorials in or near Pozières, of which four have relevance to the fighting covered in this volume. The five are:

The Australian 1st Division Memorial.
The Australian Memorial Pozières Mill.
The Tank Corps Memorial.
The Mouquet Farm Australian Memorial.
The King's Royal Rifle Corps Memorial.

The Australian 1st Division Memorial

The memorial is situated at the southern end of Pozières village just off the D 929 close to the site of Gibraltar. It is well signposted from the main road. It is a large obelisk surrounded by an area of garden. A bronze plaque on the front carries a dedication and above it is a bronze replica of the Australian cap badge.

On the right as you go up to the memorial is a bronze map unveiled in 1993 by the then Minister of Veterans Affairs, the Honourable John Faulkner. It shows the main places where the Australians fought and gives a brief description of the fighting around Pozières together with the casualty figures, for both sides, in the Somme battle. It also refers to the friendship that still exists between France and Australia as a result of the war.

The Australian Memorial Pozières Mill

This memorial is at the northern end of the village on what was the highest point on the battlefield, the windmill, on the D929 road from Albert to Bapaume. A path of stone slabs leads to the remains of the windmill, a mound just as it was when captured by the Australians in 1916. There is also a bronze map, similar to the one at the 1st Division

Unveiling of the 1st Anzac Division Memorial, Pozières, 8 September 1917 by General Birdwood. IWM Q 2601

One of the most famous of war-time landmarks was the windmill at Pozières, but to-day all that remains to indicate the site is the few flat stones and debris here illustrated. It was along the historic ridge that the 1st Australian Division attacked by day and night in July and August 1916. The windmill site was won on August 4.

Memorial, which was unveiled in 1993 by Lieutenant-General J.C. Grey A.O. Chief of the Australian General Staff.

When visiting this memorial it is worth stopping to consider the magnificent view that a German observer had of all that moved in the British lines below.

The Tank Corps Memorial

This memorial is on the opposite side of the road for the Australian 2nd Division memorial and can conveniently be visited at the same time. Care is needed when crossing the very busy road! Tanks were first used on the 15 September 1916 in the Battle of Flers-Courcelette. It is a simple memorial with four model tanks, one of which carries bullet damage from action during the Second World War. Note the use of tank parts to create the bollards and chains protecting the memorial.

The Tank Corps Memorial 1997.

The Tank Corps Memorial, Pozieres. This photograph was taken in 1922, when the dreary battlefield of the Somme was still raw and abounding in relics.

Mouquet Farm Australian Memorial

This is a new memorial which was unveiled by the Australian Deputy Prime Minister, the Honourable Tim Fischer, on 10 September 1997. The plaque is similar to the ones added to other Memorials in 1993. It stands at the end of the track running to Mouquet Farm from the D73 road, very close to what was point 54 on the trench maps of 1916.

The King's Royal Rifle Corps Memorial

As already noted the units commemorated on this memorial are not ones which have featured elsewhere in the narrative. In fact the Regiment played very little part in actions in the vicinity and the position of the memorial probably owes more to the existence of high ground on a main road than to anything else. It is situated on the D929 at the southern end of Pozières village on the other side of the road from the Australian 1st Division Memorial. It is a simple cross with a red inscription which reads:

> *To the memory of officers*
> *and men who gave their lives on the*
> *battlefields of France fighting*
> *in the cause of liberty and justice*

As you look south beyond the memorial there are good views across to Bazentin and Mametz Woods.

Graves in O.G. 1. Pozières in October, 1917. The crosses were erected by the Graves Registration units.

Chapter Eight

BATTLEFIELD TOURS

Introduction

The Pozières battlefield is quite a compact one although, like many battlefields, it spreads over more than one map! Most of the principal features may be readily reached either on foot or by car. From almost any part of the battlefield the communications mast opposite the site of the windmill can be seen and is therefore a good point of reference. Other features such as the Thiepval Memorial, Pozières church and the Australian 1st Division Memorial also serve as useful markers. The land is fairly open with little or no cover. Therefore, if walking the ground, come with clothing suitable for all weathers, particularly a hat, against the cold winds in winter and the sun in summer. Heavy shoes or preferably boots are advisable as the ground can be rough and muddy. A supply of

The main street, looking from the corner near the church towards the Windmill and Bapaume.

The badly shelled road to Bapaume through Pozieres 20 September 1916. The view is (from the Centre Way) towards the Windmill. This is the same street as shown in the photograph on the right. A communication trench is shown in the foreground.
IWM Q 1086

liquid, either hot or cold is also to be advocated.

Pozières is on the main Albert to Bapaume road, the D929, which is extremely busy. Heavy lorries and cars come from both directions at high speeds so great care should be taken when crossing or walking along the D929. If intending to walk you will need to park your car and suitable places have been suggested, but take care to ensure that you do not obstruct agricultural vehicles. Do not leave valuables on view. Put them out of sight, or better in the boot, to avoid temptation.

Before embarking on any of the walks a tour around the area by car, coach or bicycle is useful. It allows you to get an overall impression of the lie of the land, the relative positions of some of the more important sites and the distances between. For some people this tour, together with visits to the memorials and cemeteries, may be sufficient. But walking, at least a little of the ground, in the footsteps of the men often gives a clearer view of what they had to contend with. Even short distances over the undulating land of the Somme can give very different perspectives of the ground to be attacked or defended.

In addition to the maps in this book the ones to use are the IGN (Institut Gèographique National) Blue Series 1: 25 000. These may be purchased in England at good booksellers or by members of the Western Front Association from the association marketing officer. They are usually available in France at supermarkets such as Cedico in Bapaume or in 'Maison de la Press' shops. There is one in the square in front of the Basilica in Albert. To cover the whole of the Pozières battlefield you will require three maps; 2407 E (Bapaume), 2408 O (Albert) and 2408 E (Bray-sur-Somme).

For ease of reference, points of interest in the tours are referred to by the trench map references given in the main text.

Pozières village looking south-west. AERIAL PHOTOGRAPH NIGEL CAVE

| D147 CONTALMAISON | TRACK TO CHALK PIT | AUSTRALIAN 1ST DIVISION MEMORIAL | POZIERES MILITARY CEMETRY & MEMORIAL | POZIÈRES CEMET |

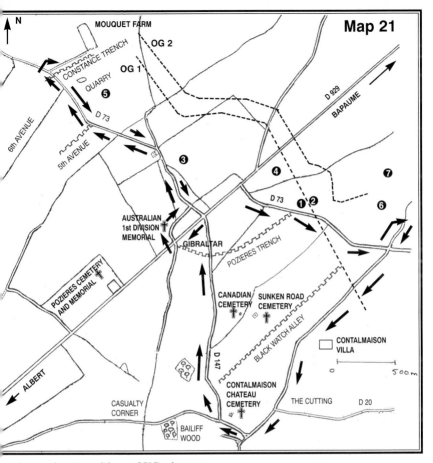

Map 21

Approximate positions of VC winners:
1. Leak 2. Blackburn 3. Cooke 4. Castleton 5. O'Meara 6. Short 7. Clarke

A GENERAL TOUR OF THE POZIÈRES BATTLEFIELD

Maps: IGN Blue Series 2407 E Bapaume and 2408 E Bray-sur-Somme. **Map 21**

If entering Pozières on the D 929 from Albert pass the D 147 on the right hand side of the road, signposted to Contalmaison and continue to the D 73 also on the right, signposted to Bazentin. Turn right on to this road. If entering from the direction of Bapaume turn left on to the D 73. On the IGN map the first section of this road is referred to as the D20. Almost at once on the left hand side is a track going up to the lines of OG 1 and OG 2 the position of which can be gauged by reference to the communications mast. Continue along the D 73 until you come to a track on the right hand side. Stop here and park on the entrance to the track. Looking back along the road, OG 1 came down from the high ground, crossed the road and then crossed the track about a hundred metres ahead of you. Pozières Trench ran along behind the village from opposite the Australian 1st Division Memorial to join OG 1 just before it crossed the road. OG 2 ran on the other side of the road and eventually crossed about three hundred and fifty metres further along the D 73. Munster Alley ran at right angles to OG 2 in the ground to your right looking back along the D 73. Where Pozières Trench joined OG 1 Arthur Blackburn won his VC and in an adjacent communication trench John Leak won the same decoration. The track was part of the British Front Line for the attack on 23 July, Sunken Road Trench.

Continue along the road to the next cross road and turn left on to a length of metalled road. A short walk up the road will give you a view of the positions of Butterworth Trench and Gloster Alley in the ground to your left. which is marked as La Tuiliere on the IGN map. Return to the road and go straight across, down a sunken lane. You are now driving parallel with the main road. In the ground to your right was Black Watch Alley about half way between the road and the line of the track you looked at earlier. Continue down the road until you reach a clump of trees on the left hand side of the road. The field containing the trees is the site of Contalmaison Villa, which appears on the trench maps but was destroyed in the war and not rebuilt. In the ground at the rear of the field the remains of the villa are detectable. Drive on to pass a water tower on the right and shortly a road enters from the left, the D 20. This junction was known as The Cutting. Turn right into Contalmaison and almost immediately bear right to La Boisselle. On your right is Contalmaison Chateau Cemetery, where Short VC is buried. Take the next turning on the right the D147, and shortly you will pass the Commonwealth War Grave Commission signs to two cemeteries, Canadian No 2 and Sunken Road. These may be reached

Tramway Trench looking north-east towards OG Lines.

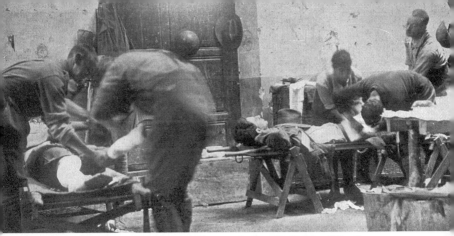

Wounded being dressed at Bécourt Chateau during the Battle of Pozières. The Chateau, at the time of this photograph, was occupied by a field ambulance of the 2nd Australian Division and a British field ambulance.

by a walk of about 700 metres up a track on the right hand side of the road. This is the other end of the track running down from the D73. Returning to the road continue on through another section of sunken road before the Pozières Cemetery and Memorial becomes visible on your left. Another track enters on the right and shortly you cross the line of Pozières Trench before reaching the main road through Pozières.

Turn left on to the D929 and then turn right to pass the site of Gibraltar and the Australian 1st Division Memorial. Follow the road round past the church and turn left at the T junction. As you leave the village you will pass a track on the left, just before the cemetery, where the railway ran down from Martinpuich to Ovillers. The track does not exist on the right of the road, but if you imagine it running across the open space to join the main road just before the end of the village you are looking at the approximate line of Tramway Trench. The road past the cemetery bears to the left and the Thiepval Memorial is ahead. The two major trenches, 5th Avenue or Ration Trench and 6th Avenue or Skyline Trench, lay in the ground to your left. 5th Avenue crossed the road just in front of the next bend and 6th Avenue came in along the next track. Mouquet Farm is now on you right with the Quarry in front of it. A new memorial has recently been unveiled near the end of the road leading to the farm. Constance Trench ran along the line of the track to the farm on the Pozières side. The farm was completely destroyed and rebuilt further to the right leaving the remains of the original cellars and the dug-outs in the ground to the north. Turn round and drive back to the village. If you wish to visit the site of Casualty

Corner this can be done by retracing your steps along the D147 to Contalmaison where you turn right on to the D20. After about 700 metres the road is crossed by a track. This is Casualty Corner and the casualty clearing station was in the ground between the road and the track going off to the right. The Chalk Pit can be visited by walking up the same track on the right. Carry on down the D20 to rejoin the D929 at La Boisselle. As you do so you will pass Gordon Dump Cemetery in the field on your left.

Walk Number 1: Mouquet Farm and its environs

Walk time 2-3 hours.
Maps: IGN Blue Series 2407 E Bapaume. **Maps 22 and 13 to 20.**

Drive to the centre of Pozières village on the D929. If approaching from the direction of Albert turn left on to the D73 signposted to Thiepval. (If coming from the direction of Bapaume turn right.) Follow the road as far as the cemetery, which marks the end of the village. This is a convenient spot at which to leave your car and proceed on foot. Follow the D73 from the cemetery and bear left keeping the Thiepval Memorial in view. After a few minutes you will reach point 84,where a track crosses the road. This is the track referred to as the Courcelette Track on Official History maps. Turn right on to the track and continue past the bend (point 85). Just before a metalled road comes in from the right was point 95 from where, in 1916, a track ran directly to Mouquet

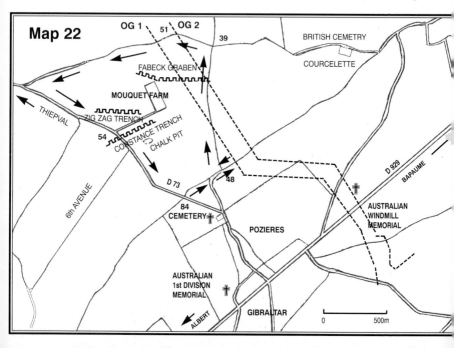

POZIERES CHURCH AUSTRALIAN 1st DIVISION MEMORIAL

TOM'S CUT

Approximate line of Tom's Cut from point 48 in Brind's Road.

A stretcher-bearing party of the 2nd Australian Division bringing a wounded man, under the white flag, from before Mouquet Farm into Pozières. The photograph was taken in Brind's Road, on 28th August, 1916. Parties with this flag were not usually fired on at this time by German snipers.

Farm. This track is no longer in existence and the line of the track from Pozières has also altered slightly. Continue along what is now a metalled road - Brind's Road. Park Lane was off to your left running parallel to the Brind's Road at a distance of about 200 metres. Tom's Cut was about 150 metres to your left running parallel with Brind's Road between OG 1 and the track up from the Pozières cemetery. At about point 48 the metalled road ceases. Ignore the track on the left and continue until you reach the crest. At this point you are standing

View of Mouquet Farm and the Quarry. AERIAL PHOTOGRAPH TREVOR PIDGEON

MOUQUET FARM

ZIG ZAG TRENCH

CONSTANCE TRENCH

QUARRY

approximately on the line of OG 2. In the open fields to your right were the Elbow and the site of Jacka's action. If the visibility is good an excellent all round view of the battlefield is possible from this position as it was to the Germans in 1916.

The track now drops down towards Courcelette. Retrace your steps to point 48 and take the track off to the right (the one you ignored earlier). Half way between OG 2 and the turn to the right was the German strongpoint which decimated the Australian 22nd Battalion and killed Major M Mackay but which was eventually captured by the 23rd Battalion. Continue along the track when Mouquet Farm will appear on your left at 11 o'clock and the quarry at 10 o'clock.

As you round the bend in the track almost directly in front of you is a small horseshoe of trees. This is all that remains of the rectangle of trees which appeared on the trench maps to the south-east of the farm. As it was, in 1916, the early part of the track is slightly sunken and at the end of this sunken section was the point where Park Lane crossed it. The track now rises to another clump of trees - point 34. In 1916 a track, no longer in existence, ran from near point 54, round in front of the quarry and the rectangle of trees, to cross the track you are following at point 34. It then went on to Courcelette. A major trench also ran from point 34 around the north side of the rectangle to join the track from point 95 to Mouquet Farm at point 55.

Carry on past point 34 and, as the track bends away to the right, Mouquet Farm is on the left. The site of the farm in 1916 was in the trees in front of the present building. It was impossible to rebuild it in the same position due to the cellars and dugouts underneath. However, the farm is still owned by M. Gonse and worked by M.Vanderdriessche, as did their respective families in 1916. The farm was known to the British troops as 'Mucky Farm' and to the Australians as 'Moo-Cow Farm'. Both the OG Lines crossed the track between point 34 and point 22 and continued in a north-westerly direction towards the Zollern and the Stuff Redoubts. The length of track between points 22 and 34 was known to the Germans as Süd V and there is still evidence of 'the sunken road in Süd V' which often appears in the German accounts.

Continuing up from point 22 for about 120 metres brings you to the point where the Fabeck Graben, running from east to west, crossed the

Track from point 48 towards points 34 and 39.

track and both OG Lines before passing north of the farm and going on in a north-westerly direction. Approximately half way between you position and the farm was point 73, the site of the ill-fated attack by Captain Caswell and the 1st Canadian Mounted Rifles on 15 September. Kollmann Trench went off to the right, just below the Fabeck Graben. Looking back over the line of Kollmann trench you can see the spire of Courcelette church and the Cross of Sacrifice in the Military Cemetery. After another 350 metres you will come to a cross roads, point 39, where you have two options. If you wish to visit Courcelette Military Cemetery you can do so by taking the turning to the right which leads to the cemetery and the village. The route taken by the modern track differs very slightly from the line shown on the trench maps. This diversion will extend the length of your walk by about an hour, plus the time spent in the cemetery and or village.

If you make this diversion retrace your steps to point 39 and continue straight on or if not, turn left. The Thiepval Memorial is at 11 o'clock. The track drops gently down towards Thiepval until after about 400 metres it bears sharply to the left at what was point 51. On the IGN map the land on the right is identified as Le Bois de Pozières and it was in this area that the German strongpoint known as the Zollern Redoubt was located.

Continue along the track but, in spite of what is shown on the IGN map, no track exists running down to the farm on the left hand side. However, the track is shortly joined by another coming in from the right and becomes metalled before it joins the D73 where you turn left. The road climbs steadily for about 150 metres, at which point Mouquet Farm can be seen at 11 o'clock and the communications mast at 12 o'clock, before dropping down to where a track enters from the right.

View looking north towards Pozières village along track passing the Chalk Pit. AERIAL PHOTOGRAPH TREVOR PIDGEON

POZIERES CHURCH

D 147

AUSTRALIAN
1st DIVISION
MEMORIAL

CHALK PIT

To your left at this point ZigZag Trench ran across to the farm. Walk on up to point 54 where the main track to and from the farm joins the road. To the right of this track stands a new memorial commemorating the Australian action at Mouquet Farm. It was also at this point that Lieutenant Oscar Jones was involved in the bomb fight on 26 August 1916. Constance Trench ran just in front of the track, on the right hand side, to the farm. Opposite the quarry a track runs off to the right from the D73 and goes up over the crest of the hill. This is the line of 6th Avenue or Skyline Trench.

The road climbs steadily and then bears sharply to the left, the point at which 5th Avenue or Ration Trench came in from the right. There is now no sign of this line. A further 100 metres brings you to a cross road of tracks known in 1916 as Tulloch Corner. Carry on along the D73 and you will be back at Pozières cemetery.

Walk Number 2: The southern side of Pozières Village

Walk time 2-3 hours.
Maps: IGN Blue Series 2407 E Bapaume and 24078 E Bray-sur-Somme. **Maps 23, 5 and 6.**

Park your car at the Australian First Division Memorial, walk back to the main road, cross and set off towards the village. Pass by Le Tommy Café and bar, cross over the D147, signposted Contalmaison 2 kilometres, a further five or six minutes will bring you to a turning on the right, the D73 signposted Bazentin 3 kilometres. Take this road. Directly in front you will see a green agricultural building bearing the name Grainor.

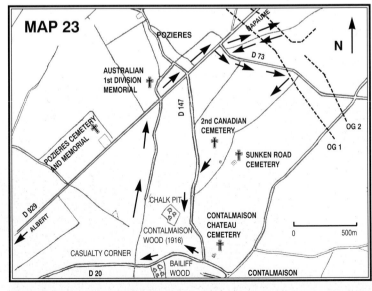

Watching the progress of the battle. His Majesty, from captured German trenches, following the attack on Pozières.

Almost at once there is a track going off on the left hand side which leads to the area where Corporal Leo Clarke won his Victoria Cross. You may wish to walk a little way up here to view the ground. The track rises steadily up to the point where OG 1 and OG 2 cross and at 11 o'clock the ever present communications mast is in front of you. The track continues to rise and when you come level with the mast on your left you are in the area crossed by OG 1 and OG 2. On your right, in the large field with the trees, is the point where Clark won his Victoria Cross.

Retrace you steps along the track, which follows the line of the light railway that came from Martinpuich and split into two lines about 150 metres from the road. The northern section crossed the main road and ran over the open land in front of the village to cross the D73 to Thiepval south of the Pozières cemetery. This railway track also defined the line of Tramway Trench. The southern track ran parallel with the main road but behind the village and on down towards La Boisselle. It was used as a reference point for the Australian attack on 23 July.

As you walk back to the road, if you look to your right up to the site

Pozieres village and the Australian Memorial at the mill. AERIAL PHOTOGRPAH
NIGEL CAVE

BAILIFF WOOD

CONTALMAISON WOOD

2nd CANADIAN CEMETERY

COMMUNICATIONS MAST

TANK CORPS MEMORIAL

SITE OF MILL

of the windmill, (Hill 160 on German maps) the ground between the mill and the road to Courcelette is the area over which the abortive German counter-attack was launched at 5.30 a.m. on 23 July.

On reaching the road turn left. The road soon bears to the left and shortly afterwards to the right. About 100 metres before the second bend was the point where OG 1 crossed the road and, shortly before that, the point where Pozières Trench crossed the road before joining OG 1 in the ground to the left. Almost immediately after the bend take the track which goes off to the right. In 1916 this junction was a crossroad, but the extension of the track towards Martinpuich no longer exists. Once on the track, if you turn and look towards the communications mast you are looking along the line of OG 2,with Munster Alley going off at right angles in the field opposite, Torr Trench ran between Munster Alley and OG 2. Turn and look down the line of the track. About 100 metres from your position the ground rises and it was here that OG 1 crossed.

The main southern Pozières defence line, Pozières Trench, ran across the road from Gibraltar, behind the village road, to join OG 1 as described above, a distance of about 450 metres. Just in front of this junction was the communication trench leading to Munster Alley where Private John Leak won his Victoria Cross. It was at the junction itself that Lieutenant Arthur Blackburn won the same decoration

Looking from the track you can also see at 1 o'clock the Pozieres Military Cemetery and Memorial. Directly ahead is a wood, Contalmaison Wood as it was called in 1916. On the modern IGN map it is not named but is by the side of the Vallèe Chavette. Do not confuse this wood with the modern Contalmaison Wood, which is now part of what in 1916 was all called Mamez Wood.

As you move down the track running almost parallel with the main road, Poziéres Trench was roughly half way between the track and the village on the right hand side and Black Watch Alley about the same distance to the left. The track itself was part of the British Front Line, Sunken Road Trench, from the junction with OG 1 until it swung right up to the main road, after about 800 metres. For the Australian attack on 23 July 3 Brigade was in Sunken Road Trench and 1 Brigade in its extension up to the road, Howitzer Avenue.

As you walk down the track the land begins to drop away and a Commonwealth War Graves cemetery is visible directly ahead but actually on the right hand side of the track. As you continue down the track you enter a hollow and the cemetery is hidden again. The track soon bears to the left and two cemeteries are now visible. The cemetery

Casualty Corner, 1 August, 1916. Men of the 5th and 6th Brigades on their way to and from Pozières.

on the left is Sunken Road cemetery and is approached along a narrow grass path running between two fields. The cemetery on the right is the Second Canadian Cemetery, Sunken Road.

On passing the cemeteries the name of the road becomes earned; on the right hand side there is no visibility whatsoever and you are well below ground level, although the left hand side drops gently away into a valley. The road continues in the sunken mode until it ends at a T junction with a metalled road, the D147. Turn left and almost immediately pass, on your left, the Commonwealth War Grave signs to the two cemeteries you have just seen. Continue up the hill, taking care with traffic at the bend almost at the top. The road you are on will shortly bring you to Contalmaison. At the T junction and large red stop sign turn right on to the D20 to La Boisselle. (If you wish to visit Contalmaison Chateau Cemetery, turn left and straight in front you will see the sign to the cemetery on the left hand side of the road). You are now walking down hill (for a change) along the infamous Contalmaison-La Boisselle road. Australians entering the line, whether from La Boisselle or up past Gordon Dump Cemetery, used this road. On your left on the skyline you get an excellent view of the Pozieres Cemetery and Memorial.

Follow the road, again taking care to cross to avoid oncoming traffic. As you drop down, the communications mast is visible at 9

POZIÈRES CEMETERY AND MEMORIAL   CASUALTY CORNER

o'clock. From the valley in front of the large clump of trees on the left can be seen the cross of Peake Wood Cemetery. The clump of trees is Bailiff Wood. Like other woods on the Somme, it is private property, but even from the road, signs can be seen of trenches and shell holes. Leaving Bailiff Wood on the left the ground begins to rise yet again. About 100 metres further on the road is crossed by a track. This is Casualty Corner, so called due to the presence here of an advanced dressing station. You are going to turn right but before doing so you may care to turn to the left and go a little way up the track to enter the field on the left and look back at the site of casualty clearing station and the Pozières Cemetery and Memorial beyond.

Return to the junction and continue upwards past Casualty Corner along a stretch of sunken road. Shortly Pozieres church comes into view directly ahead and the track opens out and the Chalk Pit is visible on the right. About half way to the pit the remains of a large concrete dugout can be found in the bank on the right hand side of the track. The chalk pit was used as headquarters by a number of units and it was here that Major-General Ingouville-Williams visited the front on 15 July. After passing two entrances to the Chalk Pit, the road again becomes sunken. Approximately two thirds of the way between the chalk pit and the main road the British front line crossed the track. On the right hand side, if the foliage is not too dense, signs can be seen of indentations where trenches and dug-outs were located. The track opens out before starting to rise to reach the main road and another stretch of sunken road known as Smyth Valley. Note the fence on the right, barbed wire using screw pickets and angle iron for support. As you near the road you can see Pozieres church on the right at 1 o'clock and at 11 o'clock the top of the cross of the King's Royal Rifle Corps Memorial. When you reach the main road the Australian 1st Division Memorial is in front of you. As you cross the road carefully, Thurnhill's gun position must have been to your left in the centre of the road.

Walk Number 3: Ovillers: 48th Division attack

Walk time 1¹/₂ - 2 hours.
Maps: IGN Blue Series 2407E Bapaume and 2408E Bray-sur-Somme.
Maps 24, 9 and 10. N.B. There are two point 66s on this walk.

Leave Albert and take the D929 to Bapaume. At La Boisselle, shortly after the turning on the right, the D20, turn left. You are now driving along the British front line on 1 July in the area occupied by

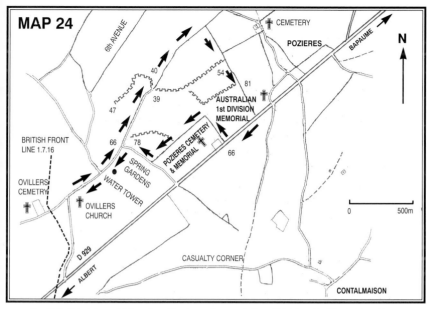

the 8th Division. Take the first turning on the right to Ovillers. In the ground between these two roads the line swung to the right before going northwards towards Thiepval. The 2nd Middlesex attacked from the ground on the right of the road you are on and the 2nd Devons on the left. Continue on the road into Ovillers village and park in the ground beside the church, then continue along the road on foot.

On your left you will pass the village war memorial which contains the name of one casualty from the Second World War, Roger Renard. Carry on past the water tower on your right after which the road bears to the right. Leave the road at this point and take the track which runs beside a large agricultural building. The junction of the road and track is point 66, and point 76 lies a short distance along this road, which you will pass on the return part of the walk. Point 78 is directly ahead of you and on the trench maps the track splits in two at point 39, about one third of the way along the present track on its way to join the D73, Pozières-Thiepval road, north-west of the Pozières village cemetery. The modern track follows the more northerly of the two tracks. The other one no longer exists. The railway which ran from Martinpuich, round in front of Pozières and thence down to Ovillers, followed the track from point 39 to point 78.

The track climbs steadily and shortly you come to point 78 from which ran trench   78-02-51-93-31-66. This trench was known as 5th Street and with the extension to point 44,was the British front line for the attack by the 48th Division on 23 July. It ran out into the ground on

135

your right initially towards the 1st Division Memorial but then dropped back towards point 66, which is beside the British Cemetery and Memorial. The track now loses its metalled surface and becomes quite rough before it bears to the right and becomes sunken with a hillock on the left hand side. You are now at point 39. The German line attacked by the 48th Division ran either side of the track at this point. If you climb on to the bank to your left you can see the ground in which lay points 23, 40, 47, 90 and 94 along with the lines of 5th and 6th Avenues. Trench 39-79-11-54 ran to you right in the direction of Pozières with trench 11-28-81-79 below it.

The 6/Gloucesters (144 Brigade) attacked points 40 and 94 from a line between point 47 and the track. When only 70 metres from their objective they were cut down by machine gun fire from points 39 and 40. Between the track and the line of the trench 02-79 the 5/Gloucesters (145 Brigade) attacked points 40 and 79 with orders to link up with 4th Ox & Bucks in trench 79-11. The initial assault failed due to a heavy enemy artillery barrage, but the ground was later won by the 1 Bucks Battalion. To the right of the 5/Gloucesters, the 4/Ox & Bucks attacked to the east of the line 93-28 their objectives being points 97 and 81 with the trench 11-28 followed by point 11; with the aid of the Royal Berks this part of the attack was successful. The triangle of ground 79-11-28 was not attacked but was deluged with fire from machine guns and mortars.

The track now climbs steadily before bearing to the right and as you climb the Thiepval Memorial becomes visible on your left at about 8 o'clock. Turn on to the track which enters from the right taking you in a direction between the First Division Memorial on the left and the British Cemetery and Memorial on the right. You will now begin to descend into a valley where lay point 54 in the German line. As you go down to point 54 Ovillers church and the water tower that you passed at the start of the walk are clearly visible on your right. K (or Western) Trench ran between the village and the track. You will also pass a track on the left hand side which runs directly up to the village cemetery. This is all that remains of the railway line down to Ovillers and the second track which ran beside it down to point 39. As you continue along the track and climb towards the main road past points 81 and 97 in the ground to your right, note the views towards Ovillers, La Boisselle and Albert. When the track reaches the main road, turn to the right towards the Pozières Cemetery and Memorial.

Walk carefully along the side of the road towards the cemetery and when you have almost reached the wall, take the track that runs to the right with Thiepval Memorial at 11 o'clock. You are now at point 66. After about 45 metres the track turns sharply to the left and heads directly for Albert. The track is fairly well covered with grass but the line is visible. Pass behind of the cemetery and memorial. The track on which you walked earlier can be seen to the right with a small valley in between, particularly marked is the section of sunken lane and the top of the Thiepval Memorial is also just visible. The track passes through the British line between points 93 and 51 and drops down on to a metalled road which appears on trench maps as Spring Gardens.

Follow the metalled road to the right towards the blue and white agricultural building. Follow the road round to rejoin the track originally taken at point 66. Walk back past point 76 and the water tower to Ovillers church and your car.

Walk Number 4: Pozières Village

Walk time 1½ hours.
Maps: IGN Blue Series 2407E Bapaume and 2408E Bray-sur-Somme. **Maps 25, 5 and 6.**

This walk will not be too arduous but will allow you to visit the important sites in and around the village of Pozières. A convenient place to park, near the centre of the village on the D929, is in front of Le Tommy restarunt owned and run by M. Dominique Zanardi and his wife Melanie.

Leave Le Tommy, turn left and walk down the road in the direction

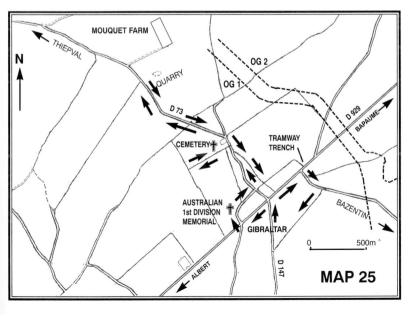

Ground crossed by Tramway Trench.

of Albert for about 200 metres. Cross the road and walk towards the Australian First Division Memorial. In front of the memorial, on the right, is the site of the German strongpoint Gibraltar. In 1991, for the 75th anniversary of the battle, the authorities cleared the site, but since then the foliage has grown back and the remains have been damaged by excavation. Wired off for reasons of safety, great care is needed if you decide to investigate further. Much argument has arisen over the the name 'Gibraltar'. The most common explanation is that the Australians were surprised to encounter German troops with Gibraltar on their cap badge, an honour granted to Hanoverian soldiers over two hundred years earlier when the House of Hanover ruled both Britain and Hanover. It has also been suggested that the name arose as the remains jutted out 'like Gibraltar'. According to Bean, for the first week or so after its capture, the name 'Cement House' was also used.

Continue to the Australian 1st Division Memorial and then follow the road round towards the centre of the village. As you turn the corner the rebuilt church is directly in front of you. When you reach the T junction at the Rue Voulleville turn left with the village war memorial on your left. On the right hand side of the road in the garden of one of the residents can be seen a vast collection of shell cases and other debris of the war. It was along this road, or what remained of it, that the Australian 8th Battalion progressed on 25th July to rendezvous with the 4th Battalion, who were bombing up K Trench. They eventually met at the cemetery. As the road continues there are orchards on the right hand side which were the scene of fierce fighting.

Just before you reach the cemetery there is a track on the left hand

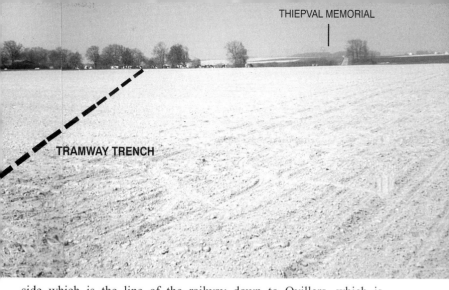

TRAMWAY TRENCH

THIEPVAL MEMORIAL

side which is the line of the railway down to Ovillers, which is described in Walk Number 3. Turn left along this track until you see another track running down beside the village to the Australian Memorial. In the ground in front of you was K Trench, running from just in front of the Australian Memorial, up to Tulloch Corner and on to join 5th Avenue near Mouquet Farm. Retrace your steps to the road and continue past the cemetery. When the road bears to the left take the road running straight on (ignore the track to the right). The ground rises steadily and eventually joins another one coming from the left. You are now on Brind's Road, Mouquet Farm is directly ahead, with the Quarry and the Thiepval Memorial on the left.

Australians returning from the trenches with their mascot.

Retrace you steps to the cemetery and looking to the left note the position of the communications mast to gauge the positions of OG1 and OG 2. At the same time you can see the route taken by the railway and Tramway Trench across the open ground to the main road. You will see the point where the railway crossed and Tramway Trench began later on. Bear left on to the Chemin du Tour de Haies which shortly becomes a track and passes behind the village. In the ground to your left, as you approach farm buildings, were the artillery dug-outs. When you reach the main road turn left and walk up the road towards Bapaume. Pass the D73 sign posted to Bazentin on your right and a sign for Fois Gras and Canard on your left. Almost immediately beside the wall there is a track, somewhat overgrown, which is where the railway crossed the road and Tramway Trench began. If you walk up to the end of the track you can see again the lines of the railway and Tramway Trench across the open ground to the cemetery. Almost certainly the cellars of the house on the left as you join the track, were the hospital dug outs used first by the Germans and afterwards by the Australians.

Return to the main road. Turn right and take the D73 on the left hand side. Follow the D73 for about 75 metres and turn right along the track which runs beside the green agricultural building. This follows the southern side of the village to join the D147. The southern limb of the railway ran between the track and the village and was used as a guide for the Australian attack on 23 July. The orchards similarly used were along the edge of the village. Pozières Trench ran down from OG 1 in the ground to your left before joining the track approximately half way along and crossing to join the main road near the 1st Division Memorial. As you walk along the track note how the land on your left

drops away. The Australians assaulting on 23 July from this ground had to do so up quite a steep incline. When you reach the road turn right on to what on the trench maps was called Polo Road, which will lead you back to the village and your car.

FURTHER READING

1. *The Official History of Australia in the War 1914-1918.* Volume III. The A.I.F. in France. C.E.W. Bean. 1928.
Also available in soft back from University of Queensland Press. 1980 A very detailed account of the fighting for Pozières and Mouquet Farm covering in excess of 400 pages. The maps, although numerous, are very small and the whole is not easy reading.
2. *Official History of the War. Military Operations in France and Belgium 1916* Volume II. Captain W. Miles Macmillan 1938.
Now available in reproduction from the Imperial War Museum/Battery Press. Covers Australian and British units engaged in and around Pozières.
3. *Pozières 1916.* Peter Charlton. Leo Cooper. 1986.
Charlton is an Australian and this account has a strong anti command bias. Nevertheless, very readable, although the maps could be more detailed and better presented.
4. *The Somme Battlefields.* Martin and Mary Middlebrook. Viking 1991.
As the cover states this is 'A Comprehensive Guide From Crècy to the Two World Wars'. A very well written and clear guide to the area with some excellent background information.
5. *Before Endeavours Fade.* A Guide to the Battlefields of the First World War. Rose Coombs. Originally published in the early 1980s but recently completely updated, covers all the important sites in both France and Belgium.
6. Major and Mrs Holt's Battlefield Guide to the Somme. Leo Cooper. 1966.
7. Other volumes in the Battleground Europe Series, particularly: *La Boisselle (Ovillers/Contalmaison)* - Michael Stedman, *Courcelette* - Paul Read and *Walking the Somme*, also Paul Reed. These cover, in greater detail, the ground adjacent to Pozières and the battles before and after the fall of Pozières and Mouquet Farm.

Selective Index